2009   3/6/20   1/00

P9-DSY-548

LIFE WITHOUT LAWYERS

The Death of Common Sense: How Law Is Suffocating America

*The Collapse of the Common Good: How America's Lawsuit Culture
Undermines Our Freedom*

LIFE WITHOUT LAWYERS

LIBERATING AMERICANS FROM
TOO MUCH LAW

PHILIP K. HOWARD

W. W. NORTON & COMPANY
*New York * London*

For information about permission to reproduce selections from this book,
write to Permissions, W. W. Norton & Company, Inc.,
500 Fifth Avenue, New York, NY 10110

For information about special discounts for bulk purchases, please contact
W. W. Norton Special Sales at specialsales@wwnorton.com or 800-233-4830

Manufacturing by RR Donnelley, Harrisonburg
Book design by Chris Welch

Library of Congress Cataloging-in-Publication Data

Howard, Philip K.
Life without lawyers : liberating Americans from too much law / Philip
K. Howard. — 1st ed.
p. cm.
Includes bibliographical references.
ISBN 978-0-393-06566-4 (hardcover)
1. Law--United States. 2. Law reform—United States. 3. Litigious
paranoia—United States. 4. Commonsense reasoning. I. Title.
KF384.H6925 2009
349.73—dc22
2008047760

W. W. Norton & Company, Inc.
500 Fifth Avenue, New York, N.Y. 10110
www.wwnorton.com

W. W. Norton & Company Ltd.
Castle House, 75/76 Wells Street, London W1T 3QT

1 2 3 4 5 6 7 8 9 0

For Alexandra,

and for Olivia, Charlotte, Lily, and Alexander,

who can make anyone an optimist

CONTENTS

LIFE WITHOUT LAWYERS

INTRODUCTION

"**S**ometimes I wonder how it came to this," a teacher in Wyoming told me, "where teachers no longer have authority to run the classroom and parents are afraid to go on field trips for fear of being sued." Thomas Jefferson might have the same question. How did the land of freedom become a legal minefield? Americans tiptoe through law all day long, avoiding any acts that might offend someone or erupt into a legal claim. Legal fears constantly divert us from doing what we think is right. A pediatrician noted that "I don't deal with patients the same way anymore. You wouldn't want to say something off the cuff that might be used against you."

Living in a free society is something we take for granted. After all, we're free to live and work where we choose. Civil libertarians are vigilant to keep government from abusing its authority. But freedom should also include the joy of spontaneity, the power of personal conviction, and the authority to use common sense—for example, to maintain order in the classroom, and to interact honestly with a patient or a co-worker.

The idea of freedom as personal power has been pushed aside

in recent decades by a new idea of freedom—where the focus is on the rights of whoever might disagree with a decision. There were good reasons why we went in this direction, but now the momentum has carried us to a point where we no longer feel free in daily interaction. Almost any encounter carries legal risk. Lawyers are everywhere, both literally—the proportion of lawyers in the workforce almost doubled between 1970 and 2000—and in our minds, sowing doubt into ordinary choices. Americans increasingly go through the day looking over their shoulders instead of where they want to go.

What's been lost is a coherent legal framework of right and wrong. A free society requires that people generally understand the scope of their freedoms. Without reliable legal boundaries, distrust will infect daily dealings. People start to fear each other, and they start to fear law. That's what's happened in America, particularly for teachers, doctors, managers, and others with responsibility.

I've written about how aspects of modern law undermine our freedoms, but diagnosing the flaws of the current system, I've learned, is not sufficient to stimulate change. In *The Death of Common Sense*, I described how detailed regulation functions like central planning—causing Mother Teresa to abandon plans to build a homeless shelter in the Bronx, for example, rather than waste money on a code-mandated elevator that no one would ever use. In my second book, *The Collapse of the Common Good*, I described how America's lawsuit culture has injected defensiveness into daily relations. The town of Oologah, Oklahoma, dismantled the double slide in the central square, the joy of children for more than fifty years, after a minor injury prompted fears of future liability. I was gratified that leaders in the White House and state capitols endorsed the message of these books, and even undertook some important reforms. On the whole, however, the status quo has proved more powerful than the frustrations.

In 2002, with the support of leaders such as Bill Bradley and Tom Kean, a group of us formed a nonpartisan organization, Common Good (www.commongood.org), with the goal of restoring reliability to American law. Common Good has succeeded in bringing broad coalitions together behind new authority structures—for example, an expert administrative court to handle malpractice claims, developed in a joint venture with the Harvard School of Public Health. Common Good is also working to design and pilot a new system of discipline for New York City schools, jointly with the United Federation of Teachers and the city's Department of Education. What we are learning with Common Good is the power of a new vision. Frustrated people are happy enough to complain, but to support change people need to see where they're going.

In this book I present a vision for a new authority structure for America in which people are free to make daily choices. Judges aspire to keep lawsuits reasonable, understanding that what people can sue for ends up defining the limits of freedom. Schools are run by the instincts and values of the humans in charge, not organized like a bureaucratic assembly line. Public choices aspire to balance for the common good, not, generally, to appease someone's demand for individual rights. Washington undergoes a hundred-year cleaning, to restore transparency and accountability. Democracy can't function if Washington is weighed down by decades of accumulated law, beyond the influence of anyone except special interests that scurry around the baseboards making sure nothing ever changes.

The proposal here is based on one overriding principle, which is this: Nothing works—not health care, not schools, not democracy, not our relationship to children, not personal fulfillment—without the freedom to exercise judgment on the spot. The power of humans must be released. Individual attributes like willpower and character must be allowed room to flourish. People need freedom to take responsibility. Accountability should be based on accomplishment, not bureaucratic conformity. We must embrace human differences, not try to stamp people out of the same legal mold. Each individual, management expert Chester Barnard observed, is "a single, unique, independent, . . . whole thing." I propose to pull law back from daily choices and give people the freedom to be themselves, drawing on their personal energy, instincts, and values. Many will succeed. Some will not. But the current overlegalized system, to varying degrees, drains us of the powers needed for accomplishment. The effects ripple through society, and virtually guarantee the failure of public institutions.

This book, in eight chapters, will describe how to rebuild coherent legal boundaries to protect an open field of free choice (Chapter 1); these boundaries define reasonable risk (Chapter 2), restrict the role of rights (Chapter 3), draw the limits of lawsuits (Chapter 4), liberate teachers and others from bureaucracy (Chapter 5), restore personal accountability (Chapter 6), revive public responsibility in Washington (Chapter 7), and make room for leadership at every level of society (Chapter 8).

Every thirty years or so America has had a basic shift in social structure. The last one was the rights revolution in the 1960s, when America faced up to racism and other forms of discrimination. Reaching back in history, there was the New Deal in the 1930s, creating social safety nets; then the Progressive era around 1900, ending laissez-faire and instituting regulation of industrial America; then the Civil War in the 1860s, abolishing slavery; then Jacksonian democracy in the 1830s, instituting populist rule; then the Republicans taking over from the Federalists just after 1800; then the American Revolution in 1776. We're overdue for a shift. The new structure will fix the excesses of the rights revolution and its false idea that law and rights can substitute for human judgment in daily dealings. Pulling law back into coherent boundaries will liberate each of us to make a difference, and allow Americans to come together to meet the challenges of our time.

CHAPTER 1

THE BOUNDARIES OF LAW

On a hot day in the Cheshire region of England in 1995, an eighteen-year-old named John Tomlinson went for a swim in the lake of a local park. Racing into the water from the beach, he dived too sharply and broke his neck on the sandy bottom. He was paralyzed for life.

The accident could have happened anywhere in America. The lawsuit could have as well. Mr. Tomlinson sued the Cheshire County Council for not doing more to protect against the accident. The council certainly knew about the risks of swimming in lakes. There were three or four near drownings every year. No Swimming signs had been posted and widely ignored for more than a decade. The popularity of the park—more than 160,000 visitors every year—made effective policing almost impossible. Fearful of liability, the Cheshire council had decided to close off the lake by dumping mud on the beaches and planting reeds. But before the reeds could be planted, Mr. Tomlinson had his accident.

As in America, the lawyer's arguments were passionate. The Cheshire council should have acted sooner, Tomlinson's lawyer argued, to prevent "luring people into a deathtrap" and to protect against a "siren call strong enough to turn stout men's hearts." The lower court accepted this argument and awarded damages because the county obviously knew the danger.

The case eventually made its way up to the highest court in Britain, the Appellate Committee of the House of Lords. Although applying the same common law principles that would apply in an American court, the British court in 2003 rendered a decision almost unheard of in America. It ordered the case to be dismissed. The lead opinion by Lord Hoffmann declared that whether a claim should be allowed hinged on not just whether an accident was foreseeable but "also the social value of the activity which gives rise to the risk." Permitting Mr. Tomlinson's claim, the law lords held, would encourage this and other parks to restrict access to normal and healthy activities, affecting the enjoyment of countless people. "[T]here is an important question of freedom at stake. It is unjust that the harmless recreation of responsible parents and children with buckets and spades on the beaches should be prohibited in order to comply with what is thought to be a legal duty."

The county's ineffective effort to prevent swimming, instead of establishing negligence, the law lords held, demonstrated how a misguided conception of justice hurts the public. "Does the law require that all trees be cut down," Lord Hobhouse asked, "because some youths may climb them and fall?" Lord Scott added, "Of course there is some risk of accidents. . . . But that is no reason for imposing a grey and dull safety regime on everyone."

The *Tomlinson* decision exposes a forgotten goal in American law—to protect our daily freedoms. What people can sue for is a key marker defining the scope of free activity. Lawsuits "often have their greatest effect," former Harvard president and law school dean Derek Bok observed, "on people who are neither parties to the litigation nor even aware that it is going on." The news in 2005 that a jury awarded $6 million to someone who had broken his leg on the sledding hill in Greenwich, Connecticut, was dismaying to town taxpayers. But it had another, broader effect—other towns soon announced that they would no longer permit winter sports on town property.

Law is vital to freedom. By enforcing norms of honesty, for example, law provides the foundation of free interaction. But law can destroy freedom as well as support it. Our founders were concerned about oppressive laws—they added the Bill of Rights precisely to prevent abuses of state power, even through duly enacted laws. Freedom—by definition, the absence of restraint—can be encroached upon from many sides. Freedom can be destroyed by tyrants, by lawlessness—and by too much law.

"The only freedom that deserves the name," John Stuart Mill famously wrote, "is that of pursuing our own good in our own way, so long as we do not attempt to deprive others of theirs. . . ." The problem with modern law is not freedom to pursue "our own good"— we can choose where we live and work—but with Mill's second feature of freedom: doing things "in our own way." In work, in play, in human relations generally, Americans increasingly do not feel free to do what they think is right, especially where there's even the slightest possibility someone might have a different view. Law has infected the spontaneity and instinct needed for both accomplishment and personal fulfillment.

We have forgotten life truths that our founders took for granted. Real people, not legal rules, make things happen. Freedom is supposed to afford a near infinity of possible choices. It is this wide range of possibility that gives freedom its power. It is the individuality of choice that gives full scope to the inner resources of each person, and gives each of us the satisfaction of knowing that we made a difference. The high priest of American culture, Ralph Waldo Emerson, saw self-reliance as the ultimate virtue of the free person. "Insist on yourself; never imitate," Emerson advised. "Trust thyself: every heart vibrates to that iron string."

Better not pluck that iron string today. Did you check the rules? Will anyone disagree? We have come to believe that law can be a kind of software program for life choices that, with enough planning, can spew out the correct or fair answer to any situation. Free choice has become freedom to do things properly, as if freedom were like checking the right box on an exam. Today Emerson's trumpet call for self-reliance is as outmoded as his nineteenth-century flourish. The person of conviction is replaced by the person of caution. When in doubt, don't.

What is needed is not a reform but a quiet revolution. This shift in approach is not about changing our goals—almost everyone I know wants a clean environment, safe workplaces, good schools, competent doctors, and laws against discrimination. The challenge is to liberate humans to accomplish these goals. This requires a sharp turn away from current legal conventions—nearly endless rules and rights designed to avoid decisions by people with responsibility—toward law that restores free exercise of judgment at every level of responsibility. We must remake our legal structures so that Americans are free again to make sense of everyday choices.

LAW EVERYWHERE

Something's amiss when a girl in kindergarten, all of forty pounds, is led away in handcuffs by police. That's what happened in the spring of 2005 in St. Petersburg, Florida. Equally strange, the whole episode was taped and shown on national television. There's the little girl, hair neatly braided, going from desk to desk, throwing books and pencils on the floor, tearing papers off the bulletin board, and methodically destroying her classroom. The assistant principal circles her, arms outstretched as if in a linebacker drill, but assiduously avoiding contact. (Why not just hold on to her? You wonder, watching . . . Is the child a hemophiliac?) The little girl is eventually steered into the principal's office, where she continues to wreak havoc on the orderly piles of paper and announcements tacked to the wall. Eventually the police arrive and handcuff the five-year-old. She screams. The tape ends.

For as long as there have been schools, teachers have had to deal with unreasonable five-year-olds. Calling the cops isn't the time-tested solution. Let's rewind the tape and handle this sensibly. Problem: temper tantrum in kindergarten classroom. Solution: Ask the girl to stop. When she refuses, hold her by the arm, preventing more destruction. If necessary, take her to another room until she calms down. Doing what's right here isn't rocket science.

But teachers in America can't do this. Taking hold of a child's arm is verboten—touching is taboo, except to prevent harm to others. So a five-year-old ends up in handcuffs.

The rule against touching a student is now pretty much universal in America. One of my daughter's college roommates, teaching beginning swimmers in East Harlem, was strictly forbidden to hold her students up in the water (to prevent drowning) until she had asked and received explicit permission from each child. She had to ask not once, but each and every time she did it. "May I put my hand on your stomach?" over and over again. The youngsters realized this made no sense. "Why do you keep asking me if you can put your hand on my stomach?" But she had been instructed never to make contact without asking the question.

Physical contact is one of those subjects that's a little touchy. We can all agree that anyone who has a tendency to act inappropriately around children should be shown the door, or put in the slammer. There are some people, as we learned with the Catholic priest scandal, who have this problem. But a blanket rule against physical contact is itself weird, almost as disturbing as contact that's a little too friendly. Young children need physical reassurance. Sometimes older children need physical restraint, or least the fear of physical restraint. Otherwise some students will flout the teacher's powerlessness.

OK, let's change the rule about physical contact. That's our instinct whenever we hear stories like this. But what would the rule say? "Appropriate conduct is acceptable"? That should be implicit in a free society. Nor do we need a rule to say that physical abuse of students is forbidden. We know that already as well. The problem is in implementation: How does law sort out what's appropriate in this or that situation?

The rule against physical contact isn't really there to protect children. The ban on touching is meant to protect teachers and schools. You bet there's a rule against any touching—doing that could get you *sued*. Teachers have had their lives ruined by grabbing hold of a misbehaving child. Josh Kaplowitz, a young college grad in the Teach for America corps, put his hand on the back of a misbehaving seventh grader to make him leave the classroom and was sued for $20 million. The parents even got him criminally indicted. After two years of hell, the criminal case was finally dropped. The lawsuit was settled with the school paying $90,000. Other teachers have had their careers ruined by an accusation not of any sexual misconduct but just of holding on to the child, or, in one case of a music teacher, of positioning a child's fingers on a flute.

No organization can function effectively unless people can make choices and someone else has responsibility to hold those people accountable. The teacher must be free to do what makes sense, including restraining disruptive students and putting an arm around a crying child. And the principal must be free to make judgments—for example, about the credibility of the student, or about whether he has a queasy feeling about the teacher. Today the principal lacks that authority, and looks to grab hold of a legal lifeline. But how can he *prove* that the conduct was appropriate, or that the teacher is creepy? So the rule, by default, is zero contact.

This dilemma can't be fixed with better rules on appropriate behavior. Nor can the problem be solved with years-long legal proceedings, complete with child witnesses and heated emotions. The problem here is with the scope of law. We ask law to do too much. It's very hard to prove or disprove whether incidental physical contact—a hug, grabbing an arm—is appropriate. Overt sexual misconduct can be proved, but law isn't good at dealing with the nuances of human behavior. Rules can't distinguish right from wrong in this context—precisely because rules lack context. Nor can lawsuits—a lawsuit accusing a teacher of inappropriate touching is itself abusive, ruining a teacher's life just by the accusation. Normal relations between adults and children are impossible under these conditions; the possibility of an accusation has put normal adult-child relations in a kind of deep freeze. The effects ripple into the school culture. Students past a certain age sense the legal fear and start challenging teacher authority. Like poisoned air, law becomes an ever-present factor in school relationships.

We must draw legal boundaries here. The only way to normalize adult-child relations is to remove law from incidental relations: No claim should be allowed without credible allegations of overt sexual misconduct. For conduct short of that, people must have the freedom deal with people as they think best—for example, by the principal's reassigning or firing the teacher about whom he has qualms.

Straining daily choices through a legal sieve basically kills the human instinct needed to get things done. Law applied to ordinary decisions leads to bad choices, which leads to more law, which leads to worse choices. Pretty soon law is everywhere, separating people from their instincts of right and wrong.

In 2007, fourteen-year-old Mariya Fatima suffered a stroke in class at Jamaica High School in Queens, New York. But no one called an ambulance for ninety minutes because a rule prohibited teachers or nurses from calling 911 without the principal's permission. (First observation: People take law seriously, even when its application is idiotic and leads to tragedy.) The rule at Jamaica High School had been instituted because of overuse of emergency calls in run-of-the-mill disciplinary situations, such as fights between students. (Second observation: Law is the culprit here as well. School officials had lost the ability to deal with disorder because law has undermined their authority by, for example, taking away their ability physically to restrain the students.) The principal instituted the rule against calling 911 because, under the objective metrics under which schools are evaluated, these emergencies were considered an indicator of bad management. (Third observation: Law readily takes a life of its own, even if inconsistent with the ultimate goals.)

After the shocking delay in calling the ambulance for Mariya Fatima, Jamaica High School changed its rule. This time it put in a four-step process specifying exactly when 911 could be called: First, the teacher must inform the nurse; second, the child's parents must be notified, and, if a parent approves, an ambulance can be summoned; third, if the nurse is unavailable, the teacher must inform an assistant principal and principal; and fourth, if the principals aren't available, the dean's office is charged with securing proper medical care. (Fourth observation: The legalistic mind-set is deeply entrenched. People trained to look to rules lack even the *idea* that they can just do what seems right. "By step four," one teacher observed, "the kid's already dead.") When the idiocy of the new rule was exposed by the *New York Daily News*, Chancellor Joel Klein stepped in and ordered the solution that was obvious from the start: There would be no rule limiting the use of 911.

Rules can't make decisions, to paraphrase the philosopher Joseph Raz, any more than a book on chess can tell you how to win. But that's the core assumption of modern law. In an effort to avoid human error, we have created legal structures based on an unspoken premise that correctness can be proved or programmed in advance.

Two great intellectual currents came together over the past century to bring America to this state of hyper-legalism. The first, which grew naturally out of the Industrial Revolution, is the idea of organizing how to do things. Frederick Winslow Taylor, the father of scientific management, preached the idea of creating systems in order to increase productivity. Organization is undeniably essential for complex products; Henry Ford's assembly lines proved that. Regulatory organization is also necessary to rein in the abuses of big business. Today we assume unquestioningly that any activity will be more effective if we detail in advance how to get the job done. That's how we've organized schools. Instead of an assembly line of machines, schools are organized by a kind of assembly line of rules. Do this and then do that, and then fill out forms that say you did what the rules required.

The second social current, which burst out of the 1960s in an explosion that still reverberates forty years later, is based on a new idea of individual rights: Let any individual who feels aggrieved bring a legal claim for almost anything. Fairness, the thinking went, would be guaranteed by letting people assert their own rights. The abuses of discrimination were long overdue for a remedy and required a dramatic shift in law. But looking at disputes as a matter of individual rights had implications far beyond patterns of discrimination. These modern rights gave undefined powers to individuals to assert claims over other free individuals. Unlike constitutional rights, which shield citizens from state power, these new rights gave citizens a sword against other free citizens. To legal thinkers in the 1960s, however, legal self-help seemed like the perfect solution to the conflicts of a diverse society. Let each defendant demonstrate why his actions were appropriate. Why didn't we think of this before?

These two great currents of social organization—prescribing rules to specify how to do things and affording individual rights to invoke a legal proceeding—now sweep us along through our day like a mighty river, causing us to cling to legal logic for ordinary daily choices. To stay afloat, we must constantly be prepared to answer this question: Can you show this was done properly? Where the rallying cry for our revolutionary forebears was "No Taxation Without Representation," today's cry is "No Decision Without Justification."

The effort to organize human behavior into legal categories has expanded lawbooks exponentially—more than 70,000 pages of new and revised rules in the *Federal Register* every year. No activity is immune. Companies develop thick manuals on what not to say and do with other employees—including such helpful tips as "Do not attempt to discuss an employee's personal problems" and, in interviews, never to ask, "Where did you grow up?" Teachers and principals basically need a law degree. A study in 2004 by Common Good of all the legal requirements imposed on public schools in New York City found more than sixty sources of law—from internal regulations by the city education department to federal laws dealing with immigration and with teacher certification. Suspending a disorderly student for a few days triggers dozens of legal steps and considerations, including, if the parents demand them, formal hearings and several levels of appeals.

All this law has provided ample fodder for late night comedians, who regale us with the latest legal idiocy. No one could make up stories like the first-grade boy in North Carolina suspended for sexual harassment when he kissed a first-grade girl. E-mails fly around the country with stories of crazy lawsuits, many of which never happened but are nonetheless believable in a legal system disconnected from accepted norms of right and wrong. People behave in genuinely bizarre ways. The warning labels that manufacturers plaster all over products are priceless. There's a "wacky warning contest" every year that gives prizes to the stupidest labels—for a letter opener, "Caution: Safety Goggles Recommended." My favorite is the fourth-place winner in 2003—a five-inch fishing lure, with three-pronged hook, with the following legend on its side: "Harmful if swallowed."

The totality of stupid rules and lawsuits does not come close, however, to describing the effects of the modern legal order. It has changed our society. In this new legalistic culture, people no longer look inside themselves to do what's right. Instead they focus on possible legal implications. What if something happens? How will you justify your decision?

Defensiveness has swept over the culture like a giant wave, drenching daily choices in cold water. Doctors routinely order tests and procedures that they don't believe are needed—squandering so many billions, according to some estimates, that the waste could provide health insurance to the forty-seven million Americans who are uninsured. Hardly any disagreement in the workplace is far from the threat of a possible discrimination claim. Teachers and principals spend their days filling out forms and "making the record clear," just to show they've been attentive to legal concerns. Authority has been turned upside down. A 2004 survey by Public Agenda found that 78 percent of middle and high school teachers in America have been threatened with lawsuits or accused of violations of rights by their students. Legal fear ripples through society—instead of acting sensibly, Americans do what seems safest legally. Simple pleasures become suspect. In 2006 the school system in Broward County, Florida, banned students from running at recess. Other schools have banned the game of tag.

From time to time reformers try to simplify all this law. But most rules by themselves seem reasonable, and have their own logic. The effort to rationalize them is a little like pruning the jungle. You can cut some back, but then they tend to grow back elsewhere. Once you accept the idea that choices need to be justified through a structure of rules and processes to govern how to do something, the game is lost. Law engulfs our daily lives.

All these rules and rights, we're told, are just the price of living in a crowded society, necessary to ensure fairness and to make the institutions of society work properly. Maybe things were simpler for our pioneer forefathers, but modern society is diverse, with many different values. Detailed legal codes and processes are needed to keep society in working order.

But the institutions of modern society are not in working order. Schools have been in a steady decline for decades. Reforms are passed almost every year, with little or no effect. Health care is like a nervous breakdown in slow motion. Costs are out of control, leaving millions without insurance and driving companies with obligations to care for retirees to the brink of bankruptcy.

Humans tend to accept legal structures, just as we accept the location of roads and other infrastructure and make our way through the day using whatever paths are available. We still have choices enough in our jobs and in our pleasures to support ourselves and to keep our sanity. But if you zoom away from the earth and look at the patterns of modern life from above, you'll see a culture in which countless important goals, both private and public, are not accomplished because modern law has diverted sensible choices into self-protection. As our individual freedom wanes, so does our sense of purpose—people increasingly feel they can't make a difference.

We have it backwards. The legal shackles that frustrate teachers, doctors, and managers in daily dealings are not the inevitable price of a working social order. Modern law is a main cause of the decline of our social order. Schools and hospitals are failing in part because the people within them no longer feel free to make decisions to make them work.

America indeed is in a crisis—a crisis of individual freedom. We have lost the idea, at every level of public life, that people can grab hold of a problem and fix it. We have become a culture of rule followers, driven to frame every solution in terms of existing law or possible legal risk. Gradually, without noticing when it happened, we've lost our ability to make the choices needed to run a society.

REBUILDING THE BOUNDARIES OF FREEDOM

The story of America, retold many times, is that it unlocked human potential. You can try anything. You can do it your way. You can . . . is the theme that resonates through American history. This belief in individual power, so different from the feudal cultures of Europe, was forged in the challenges faced by pioneers. Frederick Jackson Turner, in his famous description of America's character, referred to it this way: "That practical, inventive turn of mind, quick to find expedients; . . . all that restless nervous energy; that dominant individualism, working for good and for evil, and withal that buoyancy and exuberance which comes from freedom."

Harry Evans's collection of short biographies of innovators, *They Made America*, is a testament to the power of personal initiative in America. Orville and Wilbur Wright come alive in their bicycle shop, tinkering with new ideas and rebounding from failures. No longer wooden figures in history books, they compete to achieve manned flight against the world's leading scientists, not by scientific calculation but by trial and error. They unlock the secrets of aerodynamics by rigging foils on the front of a bicycle and riding around Akron to see which has greater lift. After they succeed at Kitty Hawk, most people still don't believe them. The scene at Le Mans racetrack in Paris in 1908, the grandstand filled with doubters waiting to see the Americans fail—dubbed by the French press as *le bluff*—is itself worth the legend. When Wilbur Wright takes off from the infield, they gasp. When he makes the machine turn— *turning in the air* around the racetrack oval—it is clear to the French, and to the world, that a couple of bicycle mechanics from Akron have forever changed human transportation.

Flipping through our national album, the impression that repeats itself is that of the remarkable power of individuals to make things happen. The force of individual willpower practically pops off the page, as if little hurricanes were bottled up inside certain humans. Thomas Edison's technique was not analytical brilliance—he had only three years of formal schooling—but he was perhaps history's greatest master of trial and error. "Nothing that's any good works by itself," Edison said. "You got to make the damn thing work."

A few traits of the American brand of freedom stand out. One is a belief in personal resourcefulness. Hugh Aaron tells the story of his father: "At 18, he became a telegrapher when the field was at the cutting edge of communications. He thought his future was assured—until the arrival of teletype machines in the late 1920s. Then, finding he had mechanical abilities, he created a niche for himself by learning how to service the machines. Eventually, in the depressed 1930s, as telephone and radio replaced teletype, he opened an upholstering shop. . . . Seeing the trend, he had learned the trade working days while supporting his family as night manager at the telegraph office." "I can attribute our successes, small though they were," Aaron concludes, "to our willingness to adapt and learn again and again."

Another trait of what is sometimes referred to as "American exceptionalism" is the belief in social mobility rather than status. People can strive to get somewhere. Immigrants understand this better than anyone. "Here a man can go as far as his abilities will carry him," Edward Bok wrote in *The Americanization of Edward Bok*. "No traditions hamper him; no limitations are set except those within himself." Immigrants in fact constantly battled against barriers erected by the establishment, but they were free to do battle, and the marketplace generally decided who won.

Finally, a belief in the uniqueness of each individual encouraged people to find fulfillment in their own interests, skills, and values. Marilyn Whirry, who was National Teacher of the Year in 2000, did not intend to be a teacher. But she was required to teach a class at a high school as a condition of a scholarship. "At first I was grumpy about it. But once I started teaching, something magnificent happened. It was like an epiphany. I found I could relate to people, I found I could excite them and give them some joy of learning. I found they responded to me. And fortunately for me I never left the classroom again."

Growing up in the South, I remember wondering how people found a sense of purpose in their lives. It was hard to see much originality underneath all those southern manners. It was as if everyone were stamped out of a politeness mold. Then, at eighteen, I was picked out of the summer lawn-mowing brigade at the Oak Ridge National Lab and assigned to be a junior researcher to a small group of scientists led by Eugene Wigner, a Hungarian émigré and Nobel laureate. They explored ideas, all day long, even over sandwiches at lunch—about the effects of nuclear war, about bioterrorism, about economic recovery following disasters. They didn't care where the ideas came from—even from a college student, and I ended up co-authoring a monograph on postwar economic recovery. Three summers with Dr. Wigner and his colleagues put to rest any doubts I had about my opportunities to reach inside myself and offer something that was uniquely mine.

This freedom to be yourself—to have personal ownership of your choices—is, for my money, the greatest gift of the American culture. Self-determination has long been recognized, by theologians, management experts, psychiatrists, and sensible people of all stripes, as the surest path to personal fulfillment. People with this sense of ownership of daily choices readily acquire a sense of ownership of the community as well; this is seen in the tradition of barn raisings, Grange halls, and Rotary clubs. In America people could make a difference.

But this American exuberance, born of individual drive, is fading. Teachers who feel a sense of ownership of the classroom, like Marilyn Whirry, are increasingly hard to come by. In talks with teachers around the country, the dominant feeling is one of powerlessness. "There's no correlation with what's best for kids," said Phil Anzalone, a teacher on Long Island. "They just tell you, 'This is what you're going to do.' " The spirit of community ownership has also faded—a 2006 Kettering Foundation report found that many Americans "have become consumers in the democracy instead of its citizen-proprietors." It's as if we pulled the plug, and the American spark is now generated mainly by people who, for their own reasons, are highly motivated—immigrants, for example, or people with unique skills and vision, such as Bill Gates, Steve Jobs, and Oprah Winfrey.

American exceptionalism is fading, not because we rejected the explicit credo of our culture—the belief in the power of the individual. Indeed, much of modern law is advanced in the name of individual rights. What changed is that the scope of law now stifles our freedom of self-invention. The American difference is not civil liberties or democratic rights—other cultures have come to have similar legal rights—but the fact that other societies are constrained by the yoke of cultural constraints about people's place in society. In Europe, Tocqueville noted, people consider themselves a kind of tenant, . . . without the feeling of ownership." All services and activities of the community, even the ability to respond to immediate threats, are the responsibility of a "powerful stranger called the government." As they went through the day, and through life, Europeans were constrained by self-consciousness about their place in society.

Americans didn't have this self-consciousness or sense of personal limits. People just forged ahead. Damn the torpedoes and all that. Charles Dickens, in his travelogue about his trip to America in 1842, is fascinated by this aspect of American character. He describes locomotive engineers speeding far beyond reason, to the glee of the passengers. He is in awe of Boston institutions dedicated to social work, such as the Perkins Institute for the Blind, established with the help of wealthy individuals determined to live their faith. Americans followed their nose, doing what they *felt* like doing.

Better than any society in history, America shed the baggage of cultural self-consciousness and let people access everything that was in them. Americans acted; they didn't wring their hands about how to act. They looked ahead, not over their shoulders. It is spontaneity, as Emerson suggested, that "makes the moment great."

The evil of modern American law is not that it addresses the wrong goals—by and large it addresses the right goals. Nor is it the undisputable fact that law has become absurdly dense—although this surely must be addressed, and I will propose an approach for mucking out the legal stables. The evil of modern law is that it has infected daily choices with a debilitating legal self-consciousness. Americans no longer feel free to do what they feel is right. With his usual prescience, Tocqueville was concerned about taking law down to daily choices:

> I should be inclined to think freedom is less necessary in great
> things than in little ones. . . . Subjection in minor affairs . . .
> does not drive men to resistance, but it crosses them at every
> turn, till they are led to surrender the exercise of their own
> will. Thus their spirit is gradually broken and their character
> enervated. . . .

This is not a problem of degree. A culture of legal fear is not what our founders had in mind when they created the legal framework for a free society. Law is supposed to support free choice, not impede choices all day long. Slowly but surely, legal self-consciousness is killing our culture.

Here we stand, facing the challenges of the twenty-first century, without any conception of law that actually allows us to harness our personal power to meet those challenges. What's needed is to rebuild the structure of law that, while sorting out the needs of an interdependent society, revives the one essential resource that made our country so great: the power of individual freedom.

But how exactly? Arguing about the limits of law seems like trying to reverse a tidal wave—that inexorable drive toward what legal historian Lawrence Friedman calls "total justice." Fairness can readily be couched in the language of freedom. Finding a unifying theory of law that balances demands for fairness against daily freedoms seems inevitably to lead to a legal rule or process for every social interaction. Freedom has always been putty in the hands of people who can link their personal interests with a purported public goal. "We all declare for liberty," Abraham Lincoln observed, "but in using the same *word* we do not all mean the same *thing*."

Safeguarding our freedom *against* claims of fairness is not even on the table. Legal scholars who worry about freedom devote about 99 percent of their energy on civil liberties against state power, which, with a few exceptions, are generally alive and well.

If pressed, most scholars would probably say that law protects our daily freedoms by providing recourse against wrongful acts—say, breaches of contract, or crimes, or negligent acts. These are indeed vital functions of law.

But is law only a system of enforcement against wrongful acts? Any disagreement, as we see every day, can be framed in the language of legal deprivation. Give Me My Rights! It's exhausting. This one-sided focus on possible wrongdoing doesn't acknowledge the need to preserve an open field of freedom so people can live their lives. Freedom today is just whatever's left over after everyone's made their legal demands.

Freedom is not supposed to be a swamp of possible claims. Nor does freedom long survive if defined by whatever anyone chooses to argue. Freedom is a zone in which people may engage in "unobstructed action according to our will," as Jefferson put it. This zone of freedom requires a formal legal framework. This framework, largely washed away by the flood of law in the last century, consists of two principles:

- Law sets boundaries that proscribe wrongful conduct.
- These same boundaries also protect an area for free choice in all other matters.

The forgotten idea is the second principle—that law must affirmatively protect an area of free choice, including freedom from legal interference.

Law must work both ways: It must prohibit defined wrongs, and it must affirmatively protect an area of freedom. Law must provide "frontiers, not artificially drawn," as philosopher Isaiah Berlin put it, "within which men should be inviolable." It may seem novel that a judge should stand up and rule, as Lord Hoffmann did, that swimming is a reasonable risk as a matter of law. But that's how law protects freedom: It defines "the boundaries of the protected domain of all persons and organized groups," as Friedrich Hayek put it. Protecting an open field of freedom is a core precept of the rule of law. "The end of law," John Locke said, "is not to abolish or restrain, but to preserve and enlarge freedom."

This idea has been lost to our age. It is only a modest overstatement to assert that, when advancing the cause of freedom, law today is all proscription and no protection. There are no boundaries, just a moving mudbank comprised of accumulating bureaucracy and whatever claims people unilaterally choose to assert. Instead of legal dikes defining the field of freedom, our lives are flooded with laws and rules, so many that no one can possibly know them and so detailed that they operate as central planning. We are free to do what we want . . . only so long as we don't wade into this unknowable sea of rules and no one around us disagrees.

This ever-rising flood of requirements and proceedings is accepted as the way things have to be—as if the more law the better. We've gotten in the habit of thinking every decision should be justified at the demand of anyone else. Imposing legal self-consciousness on daily choices is not a formula for success, however. It's a formula for failure. Otherwise sensible people, applying legal logic, somehow come to think that it's okay to handcuff a five-year-old girl.

We will never fix our schools or make health care affordable, or reenergize democracy, or revive the can-do spirit that made America great, unless American law is rebuilt to protect freedom in our daily choices. Drawing the boundaries of reasonable risk, discussed next, is a good place to start.

CHAPTER 2

THE FREEDOM TO TAKE RISKS

T he houses on Wildemere Avenue in Milford, Connecticut, sit under the shade of towering hickory and oak trees. It's the kind of old-fashioned neighborhood where both young families and retired couples live next to one another, like a scene from a Norman Rockwell painting. You can practically see the young boy pulling his red wagon down the street.

Milford is the last place you would expect to see pushing the boundaries of social policy defining unacceptable risks of life. Since the 1960s, as we've seen, few areas of daily life have been immune from legal scrutiny. Food, drink, play, social relations of almost every sort, you name it. But the town fathers of Milford introduced a new area of legal scrutiny—nature itself.

In 2005, Una Glennon, a grandmother who lives on Wildemere Avenue, put in a pool for the enjoyment of her fourteen grandchildren. The hickory trees spread their branches all around her house. That was the problem. One of her grandchildren is allergic to nuts and can't play in the pool with the other children when the nuts are falling. Mrs. Glennon sent a letter to the mayor demanding the removal of three large hickory trees on the street near her house. What's a mayor to do? Allergy to nuts is indeed a serious risk to those who have it, and requires that parents or caretakers of children always carry a shot of epinephrine to counteract the reaction when there is unintended exposure. On the other hand, the neighbors on Wildemere Avenue weren't happy at the prospect of leaving a gap in the middle of the block, three stumps instead of a canopy of shade.

Where do you draw the line? Public choices are not usually matters of right and wrong. They require balance and trade-offs of one sort or another—here balancing the extra effort to safeguard the child, on the one hand, against the majesty of trees rising over sixty feet above Wildemere Avenue. Deciding between competing interests is one of the main jobs of government. But how does an official decide? The philosopher John Rawls famously suggested that social choices should be made behind a "veil of ignorance," where the decider here would imagine that he could end up in the position of either a tree lover or someone with a nut allergy.

The logical implications here would probably be enough to convince me. Cutting down trees to accommodate people with allergies could be ominous news for trees that reproduce themselves with nuts—walnut, chestnut, pine, pecan, and hazelnut as well as hickory trees. About one out of 200 Americans is allergic to tree nuts. Making all their neighborhoods safe from nuts could spawn a new logging industry. And what do we do about all the other serious allergies—say, bee stings, shellfish, and pollen? Do we start a national drive to obliterate bees? Doctors say that there is no safe zone for people with severe allergies; children with an allergy have to learn to be always on their guard. Balancing the risks of allergies against nature's realities should lead us down a path toward personal caution, not obliteration of nature.

Balancing these interests is not what happened in Milford, however. In the letter to the mayor, Mrs. Glennon enclosed a letter from a doctor suggesting the possibility of dire consequences to the child. Risk to the child, no matter how remote, was enough to make the mayor capitulate. The town ordered the trees chopped down. According to the mayor, he had no choice. "It really came down to taking a risk," he said, "that the child may be sick or even die."

Risk has become a hot button in public and private decisions. Press the risk button, and discussion pretty much ends. If there's a risk, better not do it. Part of the problem, as we've seen, is fear of lawsuits. The accusation "You took a risk" is reason enough to get sued. But there's something deeper that's infected our cultural psyche. There's a compulsion to move heaven and earth to eliminate a risk even if in the clear light of day, everyone agrees that the effect is a grotesque misallocation of resources. There was a panic to require flame-resistant pajamas for children in the early 1970s—at a cost seven times greater than the cost of smoke alarms that would save the same number of lives. Then it turned out that the flame retardant was carcinogenic, and it had to be banned. Certain pesticides that result in dramatically greater safety and increased crop productivity have been banned because of minuscule cancer risks.

Humans are wired by evolution to deal with immediate risks—uh-oh, there's a saber-toothed tiger and I'd better do something about it. Human nature exaggerates this tendency for vivid risks, such as fear of shark attacks—the phenomenon identified by Nobel laureates Daniel Kahneman and Amos Tversky as the "overweighting of low probabilities." But an interdependent society presents risks at many levels; exhausting resources to deal with one risk means that we are defenseless against other risks.

Risk, by definition, is a question of trade-offs and odds—accepting one set of risks in order to accomplish something (or in order not to incur worse risks). Build a heavy car for maximum safety and it may be less affordable, as well as burn more fuel. A key role of public leadership is to sort through these risks and put resources and legal protections where they are most effective. These are the choices we refer to as public policy.

In the age of individual rights, however, American leaders have been told not to focus on the odds. Instead they focus on the effect on one person. No one wants bad things to happen to other people, but in America today we try to make public policy by looking at the effect of one situation on one person. Uncle Sam has become a kind of mad scientist, peering all day through the microscope to identify risks to individuals instead of looking at the effect on everyone. Any risk is cause for a campaign to eradicate it. With enough money and effort, we assume, we can create a world without danger or disappointment. The superfund pollution cleanup, for example, required dirt to be purified to a level where people could eat it every day and not get sick. As Justice Stephen Breyer observes in *Breaking the Vicious Circle*, redirecting those resources to vaccinating children against meningitis would have dramatically greater health effects for urban children.

Risk, unfortunately, is inherent in all life choices. Every choice involves a risk. Every movement involves a risk. Doing nothing involves risk. Crossing the street, exercising, taking a job, getting married, all involve risks. Risk is just the flip side of opportunity— do away with risk, and we lose all chance for accomplishment. Safety itself, as I discuss shortly, is impossible without risk. The question with each choice is to weigh the risks and benefits, not reflexively to avoid risk. Using the logic of Milford, we might as well enact a legal ban on nut trees. Certainly this logic was not lost on the residents of Milford. The town hall received forty calls from residents asking whether they should chop down their hickory trees.

This hair-trigger approach to risk, about as thoughtful as a scared squirrel's, makes it impossible to make coherent choices. "People seem to think that products and activities are either 'safe' or 'unsafe,' " Professor Cass Sunstein observes, "without seeing that the real questions involve probabilities." More children could be saved, Professor Sunstein notes, if we didn't spend so much on futile treatments for people who are terminally ill. Responsible choices, whether about risk or any other aspect of life, always involve trade-offs.

The mayor of Milford didn't even know how to talk about the common good. Reclaiming the vocabulary of public choice is the first hurdle here. We must learn again to talk as leaders. The rhetoric of risk avoidance must be abandoned, at least for most public decisions, and replaced by a practical discussion of trade-offs. This requires getting beyond the obsession with safety.

THE NEED TO PROMOTE RISK

The surge in childhood obesity was the topic for a panel of health care leaders convened by Health and Human Services Secretary Tommy Thompson. The trend, they agreed, is unsettling—the rate of obesity in children has tripled in two decades. One in three is overweight, and one in six is obese. The harm to these individuals is inevitable. More than 70 percent will be overweight as adults, and most of these will suffer chronic illness as a result, including heart problems and type 2 diabetes. The harm to society is also frightening: The cost of obesity today is more than $100 billion— almost enough to provide health insurance to all Americans who don't have it, or to give each teacher in America a $30,000 raise. This self-inflicted cost will only rise as obese children become obese adults.

But what do we do about it? Lecturing kids about their diet is unlikely to be effective. More responsible marketing, such as selling juice instead of soda in school vending machines, is certainly useful, but only at the margin. Banning all the things that contribute to the trend would lead to a pretty bare landscape—candy, fast food, soft drinks, bread, video games, television, the Internet . . . But most of us grew up with candy, soda, and fast food and didn't have this problem. The difference is how children spend their days. Obesity is mainly a cultural problem. Kids no longer find it fun or feel peer pressure to lead active lives.

Reversing this trend, the experts on the panel agreed, required reinstilling a culture of physical fitness. Almost fifty years ago JFK's President's Council on Youth Fitness, with the same goal, recommended installing monkey bars and other athletic equipment in playgrounds across the country. But they've all been ripped out. Why? Someone might fall and hurt himself.

Playgrounds are so boring, according to some experts, that no child over the age of four wants to go to them. Jungle gyms, merry-go-rounds, high slides, large swings, climbing ropes, even seesaws are, as they say, history. Recess in school is also not what it used to be. About 40 percent of elementary schools have eliminated or sharply curtailed recess. Dodgeball is gone. Tag has been banned in many schools.

Playgrounds are only the tip of the sedentary lifestyle. Children don't wander around the neighborhood anymore; one study found that the range of exploration from home by nine-year-olds is about 10 percent what it was in 1970. Only 15 percent of children walk or bike to school, compared to half in 1970. Kids have been taught that outside means danger—from cars, from adults, from the uncertainty of the real world; almost two-thirds of children think unknown adults pose a danger to them. The hovering parent wants control—unstructured play is too risky. "Countless communities have virtually outlawed unstructured outdoor nature play," Richard Louv observes in *Last Child in the Woods*. So what are children doing instead of wandering around, pushing their friends on swings or making mischief? Eight- to ten-year-olds spend an average of six hours per day in front of a television or computer screen. These trends, more than any others, account for the surge in obesity.

Safety is the reason for many of these changes in children's play opportunities. Ever since Ralph Nader exposed GM for making an unsafe car in the 1960s, safety has been a primary goal of public policy, right up there with individual rights. SAFETY might as well be a billboard that looms over almost any activity. AVOID

RISK is its twin. Nothing in schools or camps or home activities occurs without people first looking up at those billboards and asking themselves whether, well, something might go wrong. Amen, you might say, especially with children, our most precious assets. This cult of safety, drawing out parents' worst fears, new envelops children in America. Better not let the dear darling out alone. Who knows what might happen out on the street?

It's hard to be against safety. Regulators should certainly try to keep us safe from hidden defects. We can hardly protect ourselves against lead paint on toys and other invisible flaws of mass-market products. But the Consumer Product Safety Commission (CPSC) and other safety groups go a lot farther than hidden defects. They want to protect against any activities that involve risks. The CPSC has standards that recommend removal of "tripping hazards, like . . . tree stumps and rocks." Many other organizations, public and private, also loudly champion the cause of ever-greater safety. The National Program for Playground Safety, at the University of Northern Iowa, advises that "Children should always be supervised when playing in the outdoor environment." Professor Neil Williams, at Eastern Connecticut State College, has created a Physical Education Hall of Shame, whose inductees include dodgeball, kickball, red rover, and tag.

Focusing on safety, it's hard to know where to stop. The drive toward eliminating risk grows ever more powerful, pushed by true believers and by people terrified by legal liability. Each new risk avoided ratchets up the stakes for the next one. Broward County has put up warnings on playgrounds admonishing children not to use equipment "unless designed for your age group." That's about as effective, I suspect, as warning fish that the lure is "harmful if swallowed." But we can't help ourselves. We've become safety addicts.

Something is wrong here. The headlong drive for safety has resulted in a generation of obese children who bear not only the risk, but the near certainty, of terrible health problems.

Safety, as it turns out, is only half an idea. The right question is what we're giving up to achieve safety. A playground may be designed to be accident-free, but be so boring that children don't use it. Conversely, a playground may serve its purpose perfectly, but there will be a certainty that every once in a while, a child will be hurt. Safety and risk always involve trade-offs—of resources, of efficiency, and, especially in the case of children, of learning to manage risk.

Taking risks, it also turns out, is essential to a healthy childhood. Risk in daily activities—running around in a playground, confronting classmates at recess, climbing trees, or exploring the nearby creek—is different from hidden product flaws. Learning to deal with these challenges is part of what children need—not only physically but socially and intellectually. "The view that children must somehow be sheltered from all risks of injury is a common misperception," says Professor Joe Frost, who ran the Play and Playgrounds Research Project at the University of Texas. "In the real world, life is filled with risks—financial, physical, emotional, social—and reasonable risks are essential to a child's healthy development."

Let's start with the most obvious. Children need exercise, and traditionally they get it not mainly in organized activities but as part of their daily going and coming. To deal with the crisis of obesity, the most important change would be to revive a sense of freedom by children to wander around and do what they feel like. "Opportunities for spontaneous play may be the only requirement that young people need," observes Dr. William Dietz, a senior official on obesity at the Centers for Disease Control and Prevention.

But what is it that attracts children to running around? It's not that compulsiveness that drives many adults to the gym with clenched jaws and fierce self-discipline. What attracts children is the fun of it. It's fun to play a pickup game of baseball or tag. It's fun to test your limits on a climbing rope or jungle gym. Exploring anything, especially if you're not supposed to, is fun. What's really fun—more fun than anything—is risk. I used to climb up on the roof of the neighbor's garage (using an adjoining fence as a ladder), test my balance by walking around on the sloping roof, and then, with my heart beating fast, take the leap down to the lawn. Why did I do that? I don't know. It was fun. It was fun to experiment with different ways of cushioning my fall.

Risk is an essential attraction of a culture of physical fitness. Mandatory PE classes are OK, but they're not fun, at least not unless there's an element of risk—like dodgeball, an activity exciting (and now banned) precisely because of the somewhat sadistic attraction of hitting someone with the ball. An informal survey of children by the University of Toronto's Institute of Child Study found that "merry-go-rounds . . . anecdotally the most hated piece of playground equipment in hospital emergency rooms—topped the list of most desired bits of playground equipment." The centrifugal forces that throw kids off the merry-go-round are also the forces that make it fun. Those of us of a certain age can remember the sprinting required to get the contraption really moving. That was fun. And a lot of exercise.

Socialization skills are learned not under adult supervision but by coping with other children. "The way young people learn to interact with peers is by interacting with their peers, and the only place this is allowed to happen in schools is at recess," observes psychology professor Anthony Pelligrini. "They don't learn social skills being taught lessons in class." "Life is not always fair," notes Professor Tom Reed, an expert in early childhood education. "Things like this are learned on the playground." Dr. Stuart Brown, who led the commission trying to understand why Charles Whitman murdered fourteen people at the University of Texas in 1966, found that "his lifelong lack of play was a key factor in his homicidal actions." This was also true with other mass murderers. Dr. Brown went on to found the National Institute for Play, dedicated to understanding the cognitive and cultural benefits of play.

Being on your own is a critical component of play because, among other benefits, it makes you responsible for yourself. Responsibility, like risk, is intrinsically interesting. Instead we have trained children to believe that being on your own presents an ever-present danger of abuse by adults who are strangers. Milk cartons display photographs of abducted children, as if there's a scourge of kidnappers up from Mexico City or Manila intent on nabbing children in Akron and Atlanta. In fact, the chances of abduction by a stranger are about as small as getting hit by a meteorite, and dramatically smaller than having an accident when riding in a car with your parents. Contrary to popular wisdom, the National Crime Prevention Council advises that "If children need help—whether they're lost, being threatened by a bully, or being followed by a stranger— the safest thing for them to do in many cases is ask a stranger for help."

Perhaps the most surprising, and important, benefit of children's risk is this: Children's brains do not fully develop without the excitement and challenge of risk. A report from the American Academy of Pediatrics found that unsupervised play allows children to create and explore worlds of their own creation, helps them develop new competencies, teaches them to work in groups and to negotiate and resolve conflicts, and, perhaps most significant, is important for developing their cognitive capacity: Play "develop[s] their imagination, dexterity, and physical, cognitive, and emotional strength." Research at Baylor College of Medicine found that "children who don't play much or are rarely touched develop brains 20 percent to 30 percent smaller than normal for their age." Professor Joe Frost concludes: "Early experiences determine which neurons are to be used and which are to die, and consequently, whether the child will be brilliant or dull, confident or fearful, articulate or tongue-tied. . . . Brain development is truly a 'use it or lose it' process."

All these activities—merry-go-rounds, tag, climbing trees, wandering around on their own—involve risk. That's what's appealing. That's how kids stay healthy. That's what fires their neurons, leading to better brain development. That's how kids learn to smell danger, and to deal with difficult people. That's how kids learn confidence.

The error of the safety police was to move from protecting against hidden hazards to meddling in life activities where the risks are apparent. The most sacred of CSPC's sacred cows is that playgrounds should be covered with soft material, preferably rubber matting, to cushion the falls of the dear ones. "Asphalt and concrete are unacceptable. They do not have any shock absorbing properties. Similarly, grass and turf should not be used." It seems sensible that soft surfaces are best for toddlers who can't be expected to understand risk, and for equipment on which we expect children to be hanging upside down, like jungle gyms. But for almost everything else, the hard ground is just part of the risk calculus that kids, consciously or unconsciously, will factor into their play. I actually learned, all by myself, without any regulator's help, that concrete has no "shock absorbing properties."

I'm bracing myself for the return blast: More than 200,000 injuries per year on slides, swings, and climbing equipment! Not only that—there are fourteen deaths per year on playgrounds. I can practically hear the accusation now—that I'm in favor of kidocide, and that a generation of brain-damaged and lame children would be limping around America were it not for the vigilance of the safety police.

Yes, there are many accidents involving children on playgrounds. Whether the number is reasonable involves evaluating not only the positive benefits of risk, but also the universe of other life risks. It turns out that there are almost five times as many children's accidents in the home—over 200,000 on stairs alone, another 200,000 falling out of beds, 113,000 crashing off chairs, and almost 20,000 from falling television sets. What are the policy implications? Carrying the logic of safety to these home risks, we could mandate rubber floors, safety rails on beds, air bags on televisions, and, almost certainly, a ban on running at home.

What's going on in the child safety movement is not prudence, but something more akin to paranoia. Instead of safety, we are creating the conditions of danger: children who are not physically fit, have arrested social development, and don't have the sense or satisfaction of taking care of themselves. In the name of safety we're creating, in the words of Hara Marano, editor at large of *Psychology Today*, "a nation of wimps."

REBUILDING BOUNDARIES OF REASONABLE RISK

A wealthy society, like a wealthy person, is apt to err on the side of caution, an instinct akin to trying to protect a lead in games. But what's going on here is not the age-old tension between caution and risk. There's a third dimension of risk that never existed, at least not in ordinary daily choices, until recent decades: legal risk. In any social dealings, whether selling products, managing employees, running a classroom, or building a playground, there's a chance that someone might be hurt or offended. And in modern America that carries with it the risk of being sued.

Dealing with legal risk is different from dealing with other risks because, instead of weighing the benefits and costs of a choice, it requires focusing on the lowest common denominator. A choice might be beneficial or productive but nonetheless carry huge legal risk. The playground could be perfectly suited for its purpose, attracting tens of thousands of children to healthy activity, and still be the source of liability whenever some boy decides to launch himself off the swing and breaks his leg—as is certain to occur from time to time.

This is not a problem that takes care of itself. America has a public health crisis but doesn't know how to make the legal choices needed to let children to take the risks of growing up. We don't know how to say that sometimes things go wrong. This is an odd phenomenon, as if the adults fell on their heads and developed a kind of amnesia about how life works. The victim of an accident appears, demanding satisfaction, and we shrink back in legal fear.

Every time there's an accident—each and every time—it couldn't be easier to identify something that could have been done differently. When a six-year-old in Valparaiso, Indiana, broke his femur sliding head-first down a slide, the claim was that the school "did not provide proper supervision." Broward County decided to ban running in the playgrounds after it got a report showing that it had settled 189 playground lawsuits in the prior five years. "To say 'no running' on the playground seems crazy," said a member of the Broward County School Board, "but your feelings change when you're in a closed-door meeting with lawyers."

There's never been a time a like this in American history. Society has lost its sense of balance on ordinary life choices. Many people no longer have a clear sense of what we should allow our children to do. Once fear sets in, and common sense capsizes, nothing short of leadership can make it upright again. Here are two changes I think are required.

1. *Law must reclaim its authority to draw enforceable boundaries of reasonable risk.* Prevailing judicial orthodoxy today allows anyone to sue for almost anything—allowing any injured person, in effect, to set unilaterally the agenda on risk for the rest of society. Just allowing the claim to go to the jury sets social policy, as we will discuss shortly. Judges, legislatures, and regulators must take back the responsibility of drawing these boundaries.

2. *Create "Risk Commissions" to offer guidance on where to draw the lines.* Legislatures should set up nonpartisan risk commissions to offer guidance to courts and regulators for activities that have been most affected by legal fear, including for children's play and for physical contact with children. These risk commissions should be independent of existing safety agencies, which are dug in too deep to see the trade-offs. Standard-setting bodies are common in industry—for example, for industrial tools—and in professions such as medicine. The standards set by these bodies enjoy broad

support and are considered authoritative by courts. If legislatures don't establish these independent risk commissions, then private groups should seize the authority by building broad-based coalitions that assert standards. Common Good, working with health care and child development organizations, has begun the process of creating a playbook of guidelines for healthy play.

In 2005, U.K. Prime Minister Tony Blair gave a speech on risk in which he observed that "something is seriously awry when teachers feel unable to take children on school trips, for fear of being sued" and that "public bodies . . . act in highly risk-averse and peculiar ways." Blair called for laws to "clarify the existing common law on negligence" and for issuance of "simple guidelines" on reasonable risks. He concluded with these thoughts:

> Government cannot eliminate all risk. A risk-averse scientific community is no scientific community at all. A risk-averse business culture is no business culture at all. A risk-averse public sector will stifle creativity and deny to many the opportunities to be creative. . . . We cannot respond to every accident by trying to guarantee ever more tiny margins of safety. We cannot eliminate risk. We have to live with it, manage it. Sometimes we have to accept: no-one is to blame.

In countries across the globe, children run and play all by themselves. In India unstructured play is considered an essential tool of child development. Germany has adventure playgrounds that are stocked with scrap lumber, nails, and hammers, so children can come and build things, and then tear them down and build something else. These are the children against whom our children will be competing. Are we really protecting our children, or are we putting them at risk of failure because they lack tools of self-reliance?

"The age cries out for all the freedoms," historian Jacques

Barzun observed, "Yet it turns its back upon risk, the companion to free will." Accomplishment at all levels, as well as personal growth, requires looking at the challenges of life realistically, not succumbing to the cheap rhetoric of a safety utopia. People will disagree on where the lines will be drawn. Certainly the safety zealots will defend decades of a bubble wrap approach to child rearing. But that difference in view only underscores the need to reestablish sensible boundaries. More than at any time in recent memory, America needs legal red lights and green lights. Our freedom depends on it.

CHAPTER 3

THE AUTHORITY TO BE FAIR

The parents of the child with autism in Hartford, Connecticut, were convinced that he should be in a classroom with other students. He had shown a tendency to be violent at an early age, but by 2002, when in the seventh grade, he was unusually large and increasingly prone to violence. He began attacking other students without provocation. He kicked the teacher and, a few days later, punched her in the face. The school told the parents that he had to be removed to an environment where he couldn't injure others. Asserting their legal rights under federal law, they refused. His conduct got worse. He bragged about hitting the teacher, and started throwing furniture. The sense of urgency increased. "It is very difficult to control him while he is throwing furniture," the teacher's report stated. "He is a grave danger to other children, paraprofessionals and teachers."

The class practiced evacuation drills so that they could move quickly when the attacks started. But no one at the school had the authority to send him to a special education setting where there was more control. Under federal law, the school had to institute formal legal proceedings and receive a formal order from the judge. The parents, heedless of the terror felt by the other students, demanded that their child stay put. The teacher took a leave of absence. After almost two years of legal hearings and thousands of dollars of expense, the school finally received the final order in the spring of 2004 that the child was unsuited to be in the classroom with other students.

Fairness is an important goal for Americans. But what happened in this incident doesn't bear much resemblance to fairness. Disruption is by definition abusive, even if at the hands of someone who can't help himself. But no one in the school had the authority to weigh the needs of the individual against those of the rest of the school community—at least not without drawn-out legal proceedings. What was involved was a matter of individual rights.

Rights, we've been taught, are the ultimate tool of a free society—a guarantee of fairness. This conception of rights, as noted, is an innovation of the 1960s; people didn't used to go around talking about their rights in schools and jobs. When America took off the blinders of neglect, it saw that disabled children were ignored or locked away in awful institutions. Rights worked to break down barriers of segregation. Why not use rights to guarantee fairness in social services? In 1975 Congress passed the original special education law (now called the Individuals with Disabilities Education Act [IDEA]), giving each a child with disabilities the right to "specially designed instruction, at no cost to parents or guardians, to meet the unique needs of a handicapped child."

Rights seemed like a magic solution. Congress and the courts could be heroes, simply by tapping people with the rights wand. Not much federal money needed to be allocated (Congress currently funds less than 20 percent of special ed costs). No enforcement mechanism was generally required. That's the main feature of a right: People can enforce it themselves.

A veritable cornucopia of these new rights overflowed out of Washington in the years following the 1960s. In addition to rights for special education, Congress passed laws giving rights for "equal access" to the disabled. The Supreme Court held that pub-lic employees had the right to due process if they lost their jobs, and students had the right to due process for ordinary discipline. Civil rights laws were expanded to encompass discrimination on the basis of age, sexual orientation, religion, gender, marital status, and national origin. These new rights embodied a change in social values that was overdue. But giving unilateral power to the rights bearer to call officials onto the legal carpet has proved counterpro-ductive on many levels.

It's hard to object to anything labeled as "rights." Moral author-ity counts for a lot, and these modern rights arise out of genuine grievances—racism, sexism, and neglect of the disabled. Imagine yourself in a debate: Are you against rights for the disabled?

But isn't it curious, as Yale law professor Akhil Amar observes, that these modern rights are usually asserted in someone's own interest? The new rights give power to people to demand some-thing from other free citizens. The rights our founders gave us, by contrast, were defensive in nature; they prevented people in gov-ernment from doing things to you, like taking your home away.

A fairer society was the goal. By handing out rights, there would be no need to rely on the good faith of anyone in authority. Did it work? After a few decades of experience under this new regime of rights, the pluses and minuses are pretty apparent. With special education, on the plus side, students with disabilities now have pro-grams and personnel that are focused on learning disabilities of all types. This is an enormous achievement, not to be underestimated or removed. As I discuss below, however, other countries show similar levels of service without making them a matter of individual rights.

But the dark side of these new rights is also apparent. The first and most obvious is that other students are being hurt. What about their rights? The episode with the seventh grader in Hartford is unusual only in degree. Talk to almost any principal or teacher, and you will hear stories of special ed students who regularly dis-rupt the learning in the classroom.

Zealous special ed parents can themselves wreak havoc by pushing what they view as their rights. In a school district outside Houston, by the time a student with autism was eight years old, the parent had brought eight due process hearings objecting to the child's placement. After compromising with the parent several times, the school stood firm on its recommendations; that hearing cost the school district more than $100,000. After the parent lost, she tried home-schooling the child, but then announced that she was returning him to the school. The school's speech therapist resigned immediately. The first-grade teacher from the prior year— one of the school's best and most experienced—also announced her resignation, rather than be in the same school with that child and his parent. Her class with that student had the lowest reading scores of any she had taught—perhaps attributable to the twenty-two full days she had spent away from the class in meetings and due process hearings.

In 2004 Congress tried to give school officials more authority to deal with disruptive special ed students. But under the logic of rights, sending disorderly students out of the room wouldn't be fair if the disorderly acts were a "manifestation" of the disability—as they usually are, for example, with students with autism. "It would be unconscionable to have a national policy to allow kids to be punished," one advocate for the disabled asserted, "when the disability is something out of their control." So under the revised law, schools still go through formal hearings to get a violent student removed. In 2008, in another Houston school, the third-grade class practiced evacuation drills for the times when the student with autism lost control.

Involuntary violence in the classroom and bullying parents are only the most dramatic of the unintended consequences of special education law. Special ed constantly skews daily choices. Special education always comes to the head of the line—for the budget, for the principal's hours in the day, even for what gets taught. Deb White, a science teacher in Cody, Wyoming, was effectively ordered to dumb down her curriculum. "I had twelve students in my ninth-grade physical science class, but three had learning disabilities," Deb said, "and I was told those three students had to be able to keep up with the work. So I had to teach, in effect, a sixth-grade course. What does that do to the other kids' preparedness for advanced science?" Her husband, Bob White, also a science teacher, couldn't take his class on a nature hike because one student in a wheelchair wasn't able to go.

It is a nice trait of the American character, observed by Tocqueville, that we want everyone to have the same opportunities as others: "No novelty in the United States struck me more vividly during my stay there than the equality of conditions." But the reality, as Tocqueville also observed, is that people are very different. Some are born with disadvantages that can't be overcome, no matter how hard we try. Kurt Vonnegut once wrote a short story, "Harrison Bergeron," about a society that guaranteed everyone was equal. Those who were athletic had to wear weights; those smarter than average had radio receivers in their ears to blare harsh sounds when the brain became too active. Vonnegut's absurd society is separated from ours only by the element of parody. Ours too has the effect of pulling everyone down toward the level of the least able—where one student's disability waters down the curriculum, or disrupts the learning of the entire class.

Rights have the appearance of drawing clear legal boundaries— after all, rights certainly establish who's supposed to win. But rights don't have a limiting principle. Rights give a sword to one group to wander onto the field of freedom and, in the case of special education, to demand whatever they can imagine would be best for their child. You and I would do the same for our children. But there's no budget, and no line that says enough's enough. Law is supposed to provide knowable obligations, not give one group a blank check. "The new rhetoric of rights is less about human dignity and freedom," Professor Mary Ann Glendon observes in *Rights Talk,* "than about insistent, unending desires."

The power of labeling a legal protection a "right" is astounding. Few have the nerve to talk about the unfairness to other students, except under their breaths. Most people seem to accept the resulting tyranny as the natural order. The plight of the teachers trying to create a learning environment is virtually ignored: "It's unfortunate the [teachers and aides] had to experience all this," said an advocate for the disabled about the furniture-throwing student in Hartford, "but it's something you should be fully aware of before you enter the profession." Only one thing matters in the current state of things: Students "have rights, and those rights need to be protected."

Modern rights are not a tool of freedom, however. They are a form of tyranny, albeit well intentioned. By allowing some citizens to wield coercive power over others for their own benefit, modern rights repudiate a core precept of freedom. "[T]he only purpose for which power can be rightfully exercised over any member of a civilized community, against his will, is to prevent harm to others," John Stuart Mill explained. "His own good . . . is not a sufficient warrant." The validity of enforcing a right, according to philosopher Joseph Raz, hinges on whether by "protecting the right of that individual one protects the common good." Modern rights do the opposite. They allow the rights holder to assert state power for his own benefit, often to the disadvantage of the common good.

Rights sit high on the altar of American values. But the modern version of rights, like safety, is only half an idea. "American liberals are great," the French writer Romain Gary observed. "They've got a sense of injustice bigger than anyone else, but not much of a sense of justice." It is impossible to achieve justice in any communal activity by looking at the rights of one person without considering the effects on others. Justice Brandeis tried to warn us:

> Experience should teach us to be most on our guard to protect liberty when Government's purposes are beneficent. . . . The greatest dangers to liberty lurk in insidious encroachment by men of zeal, well-meaning but without understanding.

This is not a stable situation. People don't like being coerced. A backlash is inevitable. We must come up with another way of caring for people with special needs.

FAIRNESS THROUGH BALANCE, NOT RIGHTS

Fairness isn't this hard, or at least getting in the zone of what most people would consider fair. Let's go back to John Rawls's "veil of ignorance," where you choose what's fair while not knowing your situation in life—for example, whether you were the parents of the autistic child or the parents of one of the other children in the class.

What would you do? Perhaps the school could try allowing the autistic child to stay in the classroom. Who knows? Maybe it will work wonders. Maybe the other children will learn patience and develop an appreciation for the problems faced by others. After one violent incident, however, and certainly after two, someone should have the authority to make the obvious decision to put the disabled child back in special care. It's not fair, I believe most people would conclude, to sacrifice the learning of all the other students for the special needs of one.

But we can't make those choices today. There's one factor implicit in Rawls's formulation that's missing in the vocabulary of rights: the balancing of different interests. Rights don't allow balancing, at least not in the sense of considering different interests. It's everything for the rights holder, and everyone else gets whatever's left over. This is a serious impediment to the quest for fairness.

Balance is at the heart of almost every conception of the good society, from antiquity to the present. Aristotle's golden mean was the balance between "excess" and "defect": "Excellence, then, is a state concerned with choice, lying in a mean . . . determined by reason and in the way in which the man of practical wisdom would determine it." Every communal activity requires balance. Legislatures must balance demands from every segment of society. Teachers must balance the needs of different students. Doctors conduct triage to balance the predicament of different patients waiting for help. Judges, as we discussed in the next chapter, must balance the predicament of the victim against the needs of a free society. Look up at the symbol of Justice. There she sits, eyes blindfolded to prevent partiality, sword raised to show authority—and holding scales that are in perfect balance. Fairness is basically impossible without balance.

But how do we achieve balance? Balancing almost by definition is not a job for a machine or an objective formula. Legislatures weigh different considerations when passing laws, including the need for flexibility in implementation. For daily activities, balancing requires human judgment on the spot. The teacher has thirty students to worry about, and the principal has several hundred. They have multiple goals, including caring for special needs students, but also goals equally important, such as teaching the other students and maintaining order. Constant balancing is required. "The more societies become complex, the more difficult it is for morality to operate as a purely automatic mechanism," sociologist Emile Durkheim observed. "Circumstances are never the same, and as a result the rules of morality require intelligence in their application."

All roads lead to human judgment. Someone must have authority to make these balancing judgments. The officials doing the balancing should be accountable, of course, and important decisions can be second-guessed. But these balancing judgments can't be dictated in advance. Nor can they be "proved" in some objective way, as discussed later. Balancing, and the second guessing of balancing, always boils down to judgment of the particular person with that responsibility.

Fairness requires giving someone the job of balancing the needs of different interests. That's how it works in countries that have successful programs for caring for disabled children. In Denmark, for example, the goal is a free education for all students, including

those with special needs. The head of the school has the responsibility to make placement decisions, including whether a student
needs special classes or schooling. The headmaster must consult
with the parents and a psychological expert, who often ends up
mediating any dispute, but the final decision is still the headmaster's. Headmasters do not tolerate students who are violent, for
example, because that would not be fair to other students. Parents
can complain up the line to municipal authorities and, for students
with severe disabilities, to a national board. But there are no trial-
type proceedings. A senior government official in this area said
that he had heard of only two court cases about special needs students in his entire career.

Nor is there any particular budget allocation in Denmark for
special needs students; the municipality must provide these services out of its general school budget. This reflects a pointed policy
goal in Denmark that the municipality must always be in the position of balancing the needs of all students. If the parents want to
send the child to a special private school, they must usually pay
the difference.

This is not perfect, of course. The parents or loved ones would
always like the state to provide more. But on balance, people think
the system works fairly. There's nothing very mysterious about it.
If you or I were making it up, this is probably how we'd do it, with
the possible exception that U.S. schools may need a specific budget
allocation so that disabled students are assured of getting their fair
share.

Giving someone responsibility to balance different interests is
not exactly a novel idea. So why do we continue to tolerate the
bullying of legal rights? What keeps us from restoring balance
is not the effectiveness of this regime of rights—the disruption
caused by special education rights is hard to avoid—but distrust
of authority.

Americans can't stand the idea of people making decisions that
affect other people. Giving someone authority to make balancing

choices is almost unthinkable. Who knows what prejudices lurk inside someone's soul? We live in a diverse culture and, we're told, one person's values of right and wrong should not be imposed on someone else. We want automatic fairness.

Now we've come full circle. Fairness requires balancing, which requires human judgment. But the main point of rights is that they avoid the need for human judgment. Rights are automatic (or so we think). Rights are our antidote to unfairness by those in authority. Our official values were certainly unfair in numerous respects, as we discovered in the 1960s. But the cure for bad values is to demand good values. Trying to solve the problem by handing out rights doesn't guarantee fairness—it just pushes the needle to the other extreme, guaranteeing unfairness to the common good.

RETHINKING AUTHORITY

No one wants to return to the old days, when our treatment of the disabled and mentally ill could be best described as out of sight, out of mind. My father suffered from bipolar depression, and when I was a teenager, he was institutionalized at the Eastern State Hospital, a mental institution in Kentucky. By the time Ken Kesey's *One Flew over the Cuckoo's Nest* was published, the scenes were already familiar to me from my visits to Eastern State—the dead look in my father's eyes after shock treatments, the screaming people wandering around in semi-squalid conditions. We now, thankfully, have a different sense of our responsibilities.

The alternative to absolute rights is not absolute discretion. Humans have a bad tendency to see their options as black or white. Authority structures can be far more nuanced than that. Legislatures can establish clear public goals. They can give officials the responsibility to achieve those goals, balancing the needs of all constituencies. They can provide funding. They can give other officials oversight responsibility, including for accountability. But meeting these goals still requires judgment on the spot—deciding, for example, whether a student is too violent to be mainstreamed.

Authority is one of those subjects, like risk, that people just don't like to talk about. But in any joint enterprise decisions have to be made. These decisions are not generated by a miracle machine that guarantees wisdom and fairness, but by people—ordinary mortals—who have that responsibility. I know this is bad news. Even worse, as Lord Hoffmann explained, those choices by those in authority are essential to our freedom. If the judges don't draw the boundaries of reasonable risk as a matter of law, then pretty soon legal fear undermines our freedom. Lakes and rivers close down to public access. Fairness is similarly impossible without the authority to balance different interests.

Inevitably, people will make mistakes, or worse. Some judges will be unwise; some teachers will be unfair; some managers will be mean-spirited. When that happens, they can be held accountable up the chain of authority. But people will also make good judgments. George Washington cautioned against trying to control decisions by officials too much. "No man is a warmer advocate for proper restraints," Washington wrote, "but I have never been able to discover the propriety of placing it . . . out of the power of men to render essential services, because a possibility remains of their doing ill."

Common sense has an uphill battle here, however. Values trump facts, and distrust of authority is a core value of our culture. Americans believe that freedom means protecting people *against* authority. This is one place our political parties come together, competing to create structures that effectively prevent anyone in authority from making decisions.

Liberals focus on the predicament of the individual and believe that individual rights are the best guarantor of fairness—that any individual who feels aggrieved should have the right to invoke law to second-guess decisions by people in authority. As legal philosopher Ronald Dworkin puts it, "'Balanced' is a code for 'denied'" because the result hinges on decisions by "those in power."

Conservative ideology is explicitly based on distrust of official authority. Ronald Reagan said that "we know from experience that the 10 most frightening words in the English language are 'I'm from the Federal Government, and I'm here to help.'" If there has to be regulation, then make rules as detailed as possible; conservatives certainly don't want government officials to be free to use judgment. Conservatives see red when they think of judges drawing on their values. That's "judicial activism." Judges should apply the law mechanically.

The distrust of authority by liberals and conservatives started at opposite ends of the spectrum, with liberals distrusting business and conservatives distrusting government. But that distinction has blurred with time. Legal shackles are now a reflexive reaction to anyone with authority.

In truth, America has never figured out the relationship between authority and freedom. Throughout the history of our country, Americans have believed that authority is the enemy of freedom. The first try of our founders, the Articles of Confederation, failed for lack of authority. The second try, the Constitution, gave us a national government and individual protections against state authority. But the agrarian society of our founders didn't require much authority beyond the basics of crime, contract, and interstate commerce.

With the Industrial Revolution, society became far more interdependent, and abuses of private power far more dangerous. But our clunky ideology against government authority—the main tenet of laissez-faire—made it impossible to deal with industrial abuse. The Supreme Court in this period, sounding like Emerson, sounded the clarion call of individual freedom:

> [A person must be free] to act in such manners not inconsistent with the equal rights of others, as his judgment may dic-

> tate for the promotion of his happiness; that is, to pursue such callings and avocations as may be most suitable to develop his capacities, and give to them to their highest enjoyment.

These declarations about freedom were inspirational—at least if applied to the pioneer farmer or the tradesman setting up his shop. But the Court used this philosophy to strike down duly enacted laws for the safety of workers, ostensibly protecting the freedom of industrial companies. Letting a factory boss mangle workers "as his judgment may dictate for the promotion of his happiness" was perhaps not the freedom that Emerson had in mind.

We now see those high-blown statements about freedom as a cruel joke. The battle for humane working conditions, led by progressives such as Jacob Riis, was almost as difficult as the struggle for civil rights a half century later. The shift, long overdue, required a new legal philosophy.

Freedom could not be defined merely as protection against government authority. People needed protection from business too. Instead of facing up to the link between authority and freedom, we created structures that further eroded authority. As the twentieth century progressed, and especially after the rights revolution of the 1960s, freedom was redefined as protections against all authority, public or private. Constitutional protections such as due process, designed to protect against state power, now applied to ordinary interaction in schools and in the workplace. Anyone could challenge almost any decision.

Both the philosophy of laissez-faire and the philosophy of individual rights were cast as protections against authority. Laissez-faire, ostensibly protecting against government, led to a tyranny of the factory bosses. Individual rights, ostensibly protecting against all authority, led to a tyranny of the angry individual. Freedom was the casualty both times.

Authority is not the enemy of freedom, but its protector. Law is not supposed to be a sword against authority. Law is supposed to define the scope of proper authority. It does this by asserting authority to draw the boundaries that define the area of our freedom. Authority can certainly be abused, but ceding authority to people without common responsibility is a formula for abuse.

RESTORING AUTHORITY AND THE COMMON GOOD

Deb White, the science teacher in Cody, Wyoming, is not the kind of person who gives up easily. For fun, she takes her family camping in the nearby national forest, which happens to be a grizzly bear preserve. But, she told me, "the legalistic mind-set wears you down. . . . Recently I had a student who turned in a project late, and I took ten percent off. I then spent twenty days arguing with his father over whether I could take off points because it was late." Asked what the legal basis was of the father's argument, Deb said, "I can't even imagine. This is a project they've been working on in class for six weeks. They knew the penalty for a late paper. But there's this idea nowadays that any negative outcome must violate your rights."

The school administrator wasn't helpful. "He was kind of tiptoeing around so as to make no one angry, acting like a referee." Deb eventually gave up. "Why should I go to bed upset every night? Sure it's unfair to the other kids who somehow managed to get the work done. Sure it's a bad lesson in how to get your way. But life's too short. I said, 'Fine, I'll give him the points back.' Just give them what they want."

The rights revolution has descended pretty far since the glory days of tearing down the walls of segregation. Now teachers can't change a grade for a late paper. This is not an aberration. Sociologist Richard Arum found that almost 50 percent of teachers believed that they didn't have authority to change grades based on classroom deportment. No such legal rule in fact exists. But it doesn't matter. Rights have taken a life of their own.

Rights now exist because people believe they exist. Most people would be hard pressed to tell you what exactly these rights are. The new rights are amorphous, a kind of a catchall for protections against unfair authority. People assume that there's a right to due process on almost any decision that affects anyone—in the classroom, on the playing fields, in the workplace, you name it. Students regularly accuse teachers of violating their rights. This belief in legal rights, mainly unfounded, has become its own reality. Rights are everywhere.

Digging ourselves out of this rut is impossible without a radical change in approach. The rights have spawned a class of zealots, who assert their rights like fire-breathing dragons. Without a higher authority to protect us, we shrivel up. The only solution is to abandon the mechanism of rights altogether for daily activities. Deb White and her school principal need the authority to listen to the angry parent and then to say, politely but firmly: "Those are the rules." End of discussion. If the father followed through with his threat of suing, the judge should not only dismiss the case promptly but charge the father with all the school's costs (including the wasted time by educators).

Restoring the authority to balance changes the dynamics of public choice radically. Instead of asserting rights, the claimant must make his argument on the basis of what's reasonable. Instead of making escalating demands, the parent or other advocate now has to frame the discussion in terms of the effect on everyone else. People compete on the basis of reasonableness, not legal threats. The strident vocabulary of entitlement is replaced by one of balance and accommodation. The argument gravitates toward the center. If some parent persists in arguing that he's entitled to something, all that's needed is to kick it up the line to the person in charge of resolving disagreements. That's what authority is for.

Rights should be put back on the constitutional altar where they came from—basically, civil liberties such as free speech, property rights, or protection from systemic discrimination. Those rights do not require people to act at the insistence of the rights bearer or interfere with the balancing judgments needed to run a school or other enterprise.

It's hard for a society to shift gears, and changes in basic approach normally can't be done with too much subtlety. Rights rhetoric should basically be banned from daily disputes. What's required to put this genie back in its bottle is as simple as it is revolutionary: Restore the authority of people with responsibility to make judgments that strive toward balance. These judgments will be accountable, not by legal rights asserted by whoever is unhappy, but by judgments of others up the line.

1.   *Rewrite statutes to restore balancing authority.* Statutes that provide services or accommodations, such as special education laws, should be amended so that disagreements are resolved by officials who have that responsibility, not resolved as a matter of rights in legal hearings. A busy principal or supervisor can hardly take the time to prepare for litigation, with documents, witnesses, and emotional rancor. Moreover, as discussed later, decisions like these are matters of judgment, not proof. Just the threat of a proceeding, as with the angry father in Deb White's class, is enough to make a principal cave in. Educators and officials must have the authority to act as our surrogates in making common choices.

2.   *Abandon the due process model for social services.* The Supreme Court must do its part to remedy this overflow of rights. All the superstitions about due process in schools and public institutions need to be rejected in no uncertain terms. The Court has already moved in this direction by watering down the due process rulings. Now it needs to take the last essential step toward clarity and confirm that daily choices in schools have no constitutional overlay. Schools henceforth will be accountable by decisions of duly elected officials or their nominees, not in lawsuits.

I don't want to understate the difficulty of making this shift. Heaven help the political leader who steps out front on this problem. No group wants to give up its rights. Zealots will chain themselves to front doors and scream injustice when we try to restore balance instead of unlimited rights. Perhaps you and I too would feel this way if we shared their predicament. But the overpowering sense of entitlement doesn't make it right. Democracy aspires to balance, not zealotry.

Every culture, wittingly or unwittingly, has a public philosophy, a frame of reference by which people relate to each other. Many among us probably think that the last half of the twentieth century will go down in history as the Age of Individual Rights, or some such high-minded name. There are certainly heroes who'll get credit for breaking the bondage of racism and gender discrimination. But those triumphs may be tarnished if, in the name of rights, we lose our ability to raise healthy children or run our schools. Just as the defenders of laissez-faire hoped to be remembered as defenders of freedom, but ended up being remembered as apologists for industrial abuse, so too the age of individual rights may be remembered as a period of bullying by using law.

Our governing philosophy is not, in truth, fairly characterized as one of individual rights, except in a mutant version that removes our freedom to act. Our governing philosophy is to strive for the lowest common denominator—a belief that society will somehow achieve equilibrium if it placates whoever is complaining. Our monocular focus on the individual, like our obsession to eliminate risk, makes it impossible to achieve any of our stated goals, including fairness.

The rights revolution was doomed from the start. It didn't account for a truth of human nature—that people are wired to be self-centered. "The power of self-interest," Reinhold Niebuhr argued, colors all human activity. As Niebuhr put it, "reason is always . . . the servant of interest." Our founders understood this well. "[S]ince man was an unchangeable creature of self interest," historian Richard Hofstadter observed, our founders "would not . . . leave anything to his capacity for restraint." That's why they created a government structure that in various ways could be insulated from the passions of what they called faction. Modern rights, by giving legal powers to some groups over others, basically institutionalize faction. The effect, predictably, is to draw out the worst of human nature. Give me, give me more.

Nor did the rights revolution account for the essential truth of public choices—that legitimate interests in society always conflict. "Liberty for the wolves," as philosopher Isaiah Berlin put it, "is death to the lambs." These conflicts cannot be resolved by an automatic system of rights and duties. They require constant choices, taking into account scarce resources and other circumstances.

The decline in social responsibility couldn't have come at a worse time. We live in an age of unavoidable interdependence. Our interdependence demands not an atomized view of individual rights but a greater sense of social accommodation. We're all in it together. Health care, schools, the environment, to name three, are effectively joint goods. Every dollar wasted on unnecessary health care is a dollar not available to someone who needs it. Every hour spent by a teacher in a dispute with a parent is an hour not available for preparing or teaching. Modern society cannot fulfill all its responsibilities if its citizens are grabbing all they can.

The selfish tendencies of a rights regime are exacerbated in an anonymous society, which lacks the restraining influence of small community. In the 1980s the communitarian movement, led by sociologist Amitai Etzioni, tried to encourage a greater sense of ownership in our common choices. Sociologist Benjamin Barber now organizes a worldwide "Interdependence Day" on September 11 each year. But there's something missing that relegates communitarians to being a chorus of do-gooders. Communitarians don't have a developed theory of authority. People will always make selfish demands on common resources, for the reasons stated by Niebuhr, unless there's a mechanism that draws the line on behalf of all society.

Moving the needle back to the center—generally the goal of good public policy—requires restoring the authority for balancing. Perhaps nowhere is this authority for balancing more important than in drawing the boundaries of lawsuits, which is what we discuss next.

CHAPTER 4

THE BOUNDARIES OF LAWSUITS

n 2002 a volunteer for the Legion of Mary in Milwaukee, delivering a statue of the Virgin Mary to an ill parishioner, ran a red light and had an accident, causing an eighty-two-year-old man to become a quadriplegic. The victim sued the negligent driver. Then the victim, in search of a deep pocket, sued the Catholic Archdiocese of Milwaukee, claiming that it should be liable for the acts of volunteers of the Legion of Mary, a Catholic lay organization.

All sorts of legal red flags were raised by the claim against the church: Are nonprofit organizations liable when volunteers are driving their own cars—say, bringing a casserole to the church social, or going to coach Little League? The judge did not even address those questions. He just gave the claim to the jury. The jury then returned a verdict of $17 million against the archdiocese. More red flags. Money can't bring back the quality of life for the elderly victim. The church didn't try to hurt him; indeed, the church didn't do anything. $17 million is a lot of dollar bills in the collection plate. What about all the good works that the church will be unable to provide? Where are the legal boundaries here?

With any tragedy, like paralysis, it couldn't be easier to make an emotional argument for a huge verdict. How much would you take to be paralyzed? No amount is enough. But money won't bring back the ability to walk either. Is the point of justice to make people really rich when they suffer misfortunes? No one is making these choices on behalf of society.

Lawsuits are an essential tool of a free country. They're the mechanism by which right and wrong in particular disputes are sorted out. Lawsuits are also where citizens see the application of legal boundaries—whether swimming in a lake is a reasonable risk, for example. Lawsuits are where the rubber of social mores meets the legal road: Public choices on risk, standards of care, and exposure to damages ultimately get applied in the courtroom. What people are allowed to sue for is public policy.

How lawsuits are supposed to do this job, however, has received surprisingly little attention. Tort reformers have spent years trying to herd lawsuits into corrals that limit crazy verdicts, with success in some states. But tort reformers haven't even attempted to deal with lawsuits as manifestations of public policy, or to question how lawsuits get argued and decided.

The orthodoxy of accident lawsuits today is that no one on behalf of broader society, at least no one in the courtroom, is authorized to draw the boundaries of lawsuits. That job is given to juries. Juries are generally sensible, but they don't have the authority to act on behalf of the broader society. One jury can't bind the next. Juries can't write legal opinions drawing legal boundaries, or issue written rulings to guide behavior. Juries decide only at the conclusion of years of legal skirmishing, with no capacity to dismiss claims earlier or to put reasonable limits on claims and defenses. Juries just go thumbs up or down at the end of the particular case. The next case, on the same facts, may result in exactly the opposite verdict.

Without a deliberate legal policy of what's a reasonable risk, or what are reasonable damages, lawsuits in America are limited mainly by the imagination of the lawyers. Damages are literally arbitrary. You may be wondering how the jury in the Milwaukee car accident came up with a verdict of seventeen million dollars. Here is part of the closing argument of the plaintiff's lawyer:

> [T]here's not much worse than quadriplegia and being trapped in your body, having no freedom of movement, no ability to feed yourself, really no ability to do anything. . . . We learned about the bowel not working. . . . Then the other complications you heard about, the sores that were developed, one below the rectum which led to a lot of problems, then the sore on the leg which led to the amputation. . . . No right-thinking person would trade places with [the victim] for any amount of money, so how do you put a value on that, and yet that's the assignment you've been given by the court. . . . [M]y suggestion to you for the past pain and suffering and disability is $5 million dollars. It may be low, it may be high. . . . I can imagine as jurors that you'd like to have . . . help. "Can't the legislature or the courts or someone give us some guidance?" You don't get that. You have to figure it out. And collectively I'm sure you're up to the task. . . . [P]art of your responsibility is to determine a number [for pain and suffering] for the future; perhaps something in the range of 4 to 7 million dollars is fair. . . .

This type of emotional claim for pain and suffering—available in every human tragedy—has no connection to the concept of a fact, such as the actual monetary losses or costs of care. Just put your finger in the air and make something up, as the lawyer in Milwaukee candidly argues to the jury.

We've been taught that America has the fairest system of justice in the world. The courthouse door is open for anyone to claim almost anything. The judge, like a neutral referee, will make sure each side has its chance to argue and, after reading the legal principles to a jury, allows it to decide. The idea of the jury, a randomly picked group of citizens, is the embodiment of American fairness. It's in the Constitution.

Former Senator John Edwards, a successful plaintiff's lawyer, waxed eloquent about the virtues of this conception of justice in an essay in *Newsweek* entitled "Juries: Democracy in Action": "The people who sit on juries are the same people who decide who the president should be." Fairness in this conception is demonstrated by the absence of interference with the jury's prerogative. This is what the trial lawyers mean when they invoke, in every other breath, "the right to sue." No one can claim the deck was stacked when a jury makes the decision.

But there is another conception of justice. This other model focuses not just on fairness in the particular case but on preserving the freedom of everyone in society. Claims affect people not in the courtroom. What about the church's willingness to encourage volunteers? The goal of justice in this conception is to maintain boundaries of law. "There is an important question of freedom at stake," as the law lords held in the case of the paralyzed swimmer.

Predictability is the first value of this model; people need to know what they can be sued for. The rule of law—the very *idea* of the rule of law—is that it is supposed to set and apply standards of conduct consistently. An "essential element of the concept of justice," legal philosopher H. L. A. Hart observed, "is the principle of treating like cases alike."

It is impossible to reconcile these two ideas of justice. Under the "democracy in action" conception, each jury decides a case as it sees fit, whatever the verdict in similar prior cases. This model not only tolerates, but arguably encourages, decisions that vary wildly from case to case. Fairness is defined largely by the neutrality of a jury, not by consistency among similar cases. Indeed, if fairness were an issue only for parties in a particular case, why not let the jury make the choice?

But lawsuits affect the freedom of people not in the courtroom as well as the particular parties. Is civil justice supposed to be "democracy in action"—a series of little elections in which standards of behavior are decided jury by jury—or is it supposed be rendered by the rule of law? The rule of law model requires written rulings by judges, not ad hoc verdicts by juries.

Americans like the idea of a jury. It's easy to see the jury making decisions *within* legal boundaries. The problem is that no one is keeping claims and arguments within reasonable bounds. "An act is illegal," Professor Donald Black once observed, "if it is *vulnerable* to legal action." By that standard, in today's ad hoc conception of justice, almost any act is potentially illegal. That's why Americans no longer feel free in daily dealings.

THE ANATOMY OF LEGAL DISTRUST

In 2007 the story broke that a Washington, D.C., lawyer—actually an administrative law judge—had sued his dry cleaner for $54 million because it had allegedly lost a pair of his pants. He felt strongly that he had been wronged. "There is no case," he argued, "that comes anywhere close to the outrageousness of the behavior of the defendants." He calculated the damages on the basis of a District of Columbia $1500 consumer fraud penalty, multiplied by twelve alleged violations, multiplied by the 1,200 days he had been deprived of his pants, multiplied by the three owners. He then added $15,000 for the cost of a rental car every weekend to take his cleaning to a more reliable establishment, $542,000 for the value of the time he spent righting this wrong, and $500,000 for his "mental suffering, inconvenience and discomfort."

The lawsuit was obviously absurd. It illustrates again an important truth about human nature—that angry people can go nuts. This in turn illustrates an important point about how to run a system of justice: We can't trust people to be reasonable when they get involved in lawsuits.

What was most shocking about the case was not the idiotic claim, however, but that the case was allowed to go on for more than two years—complete with sworn testimony on how the cleaner maintained its laundry tickets and what it really meant by the sign that said "*Satisfaction Guaranteed.*" The judge expressed "significant concerns that the plaintiff is acting in bad faith" but, like most American judges, thought that his duty was to shepherd the case toward ultimate verdict after a full trial—in this case, a bench trial (i.e., without a jury) before another judge. So the fate of the defendants, a family of Korean immigrants working hard to make their way in the new country, hung in the balance until that fateful day. At the end of two years of discovery and legal wrangling, the judge trying the case had no apparent difficulty deciding that the claim was baseless.

Justice prevailed, some might say. That's basically the argument of defenders of American justice: that common sense carries the day most of the time. That's probably not the view of the dry cleaner after being dragged over the coals for two years by an obsessed person. The family spent more than $100,000 in legal fees, considered moving back to Korea, and ended up closing the store in question. An observer said they looked like they had suffered body blows, and the son's wife said her mother-in-law had "lost four dress sizes" during the ordeal. Why, they wondered, should angry people be allowed to wield this power so abusively?

The system is hardly perfect, trial lawyers will admit, but in general American justice is about as good a system as anybody could hope for. There are not many good numbers on the fairness of American justice—some studies suggest that judges generally agree with juries. The area most studied is medical malpractice. Overall, including settlements, about 25 percent of medical malpractice payments are made on claims, without merit, according to a 2006 study at the Harvard School of Public Health. (The error rate in cases involving certain specialties, such as obstetrics, is higher.) The error works in the other direction as well—the same Harvard study found that 25 percent of meritorious claims got nothing. Defenders of the status quo use this study to argue that the "medical malpractice system works pretty well."

Distrust of justice is not mainly a matter of the odds, however. It's human nature, as already noted, to overreact to terrible risks. Certainly a 25 percent chance of losing a baseless case doesn't inspire confidence—playing Russian roulette with one bullet in four chambers is not all that reassuring. But there's something else about justice that is frightening. Justice doesn't have the *goal* of being reasonable. Its main goal is to be neutral.

Encounters with American justice are a nightmare. Litigants live for years under a dark cloud of hyperbole and accusation. Plaintiffs sue for the moon almost every time—and why not? The leverage is enormous, like putting a legal gun in someone's ribs. Lawyers for guilty defendants can do the same thing, making up whatever arguments will postpone the day of reckoning. What was most revealing in the Harvard malpractice study was how inefficient the system is. The average time to settlement for patients injured by error was an astounding five years. Legal and administrative expenses consumed 54 percent of the total cost. "It would be hard to design a more inefficient compensation system," says Professor Michelle Mello, who helped lead the study, "or one which skewed incentives more away from candor and good practices."

Neutral justice, American style, is a formula for exhaustion and fear, not trust. First you argue, then they argue, year after year, until . . . if you can last that long, the right result is reached, three-quarters of the time. This system, supposedly neutral, in fact tilts the scales in favor of whoever is in the wrong. Defendants can coerce an unfair settlement by dragging their feet, and plaintiffs can extort settlements by suing for ruinous damages irrespective of actual loss or fault.

In one medical malpractice lawsuit, described by Dr. Atul Gawande in *Better*, a dermatologist ordered a biopsy on a small growth and, when the results indicated malignancy, advised the patient to remove all surrounding skin. The patient resisted, got a second opinion and biopsy which showed no malignancy, and decided not to take the first doctor's advice. Terminal cancer reappeared several years later. Before the patient died, she found a lawyer and sued the first doctor on the basis that, in a call with him after the second biopsy, he should have been more insistent. After seven years of legal battling, the doctor found himself on the witness stand being cross-examined on how many articles he had written (implying he wasn't very good if he had not published) and being grilled on why he had not taken notes on the fateful call. The doctor prevailed. But like the Korean cleaners, he felt as if a chunk of his life had been stolen from him.

Americans don't trust American justice anymore. In a 2005 poll only 16 percent of Americans said they would trust justice if someone brought a baseless claim against them. This distrust translates, more or less directly, into a loss of the sense of freedom. Americans become defensive in ordinary dealings—for example, 93 percent of Pennsylvania doctors admitted practicing defensive medicine. Nor is justice considered reliable to safeguard against misconduct— over 90 percent of Americans in the 2007 poll thought "that large corporations often get away with wrongdoing because they have the money to hire good lawyers and expert witnesses." Justice is seen not as the foundation of freedom but as a tool for self-interest. The same 2007 poll also found that 89 percent of Americans see "an increasing tendency for Americans to threaten legal action and lawsuits when things go wrong."

This pervasive distrust of justice, trial lawyers argue, is just the result of a calculated "scare campaign" by corporations. Bar associations call for "more creative ways to inform the public" about the "benefits of the jury system." It is certainly accurate that absurd claims, however unusual, make the headlines. But the most visible promoters of scary justice are the plaintiffs' lawyers themselves, barking through a megaphone of radio ads and billboards about huge rewards for common accidents. *"Get the Cash That You Deserve. Over $100 Million Recovered for Our Clients." "No It's Not a Lottery. It's Justice."*

How do we restore trust in justice? Tort reform hasn't done the trick. Limiting noneconomic damages reduces the fear factor, but a doctor who has done nothing wrong can still be dragged through years of litigation and be held liable. Public trust in justice is not built on legal caps or a better understanding of the probabilities of being sued. Trust can be built only on commitment by justice always to try to keep claims within reasonable bounds. For justice to act as the foundation of freedom, citizens must believe that it has the goal of affirmatively protecting reasonableness—both protecting against unreasonable conduct and protecting against unreasonable claims.

THE CORROSION OF THE CULTURE

The tort reform debate has tended to focus on the fairness of justice. Back and forth the argument goes: Why should someone get $17 million from the Catholic Church because a volunteer ran the red light? Why not, how would you like to be paralyzed? But there's no resolution—fairness is always in the eye of the beholder. That's one of the reasons fairness requires an independent arbiter balancing different interests. That's also why fairness is not the best way of engaging debate on issues of policy. The effects of unreliable justice on freedom, on the other hand, can be seen just by watching how people behave.

Funny things happen when people don't trust justice. They don't act sensibly. They start walking on eggshells. Legal self-consciousness creates a kind of upside-down world. Swimming, as the law lords predicted, becomes an activity to be avoided, not enjoyed. A school in Brooklyn had its beach day near Coney Island—except that the children were prohibited from going in the ocean. When hidden hazards do exist, the legal incentive pushes people to do nothing; who knows what will be enough? For years the town of Long Beach, New Jersey, had signs warning of rip tides in the area—a sensible precaution. In 2005 it removed them because, according to the town attorney, "having no signs . . . reduces the risk of being sued." He said that the town might be liable if "a jury found its signs to be inadequate." (Public outcry in Long Beach has now forced the town to engage in a rip tide awareness campaign.)

Nowhere is legal fear more corrosive than in American health care. The felt need to answer to the lowest common denominator has transformed health care delivery, with only moderate overstatement, into an exercise of self-protection.

Quality of care has suffered because of the chilling of professional interaction. Careless errors aren't caught because doctors and nurses don't speak up—asking "Are you sure that's the right prescription?" might result in legal responsibility. The Joint Commission on Accreditation reported that distrust of justice "keeps us from doing things that we, as good professionals, would naturally do." The logic of legal fear, as with warnings of rip tides in Long Beach, is that it's safer to say nothing—that way you don't take legal responsibility. Legal fear also affects whether a patient gets care—high-risk procedures may be the only way to save a life, but doctors can't be blamed if they do nothing.

Health care costs are spiraling out of control—more than $7,000 per person, compared with less than $4,000 in most Western European countries—and rising annually at unsustainable levels. Part of the difference is that America buys more heroic care. We also pay our doctors more. But some significant amount is waste. Unnecessary care—motivated by legal fear, greed, and ineffective variations in care—accounts for upwards of 30 percent of the total bill. Defensiveness seeps into daily decisions like an acid, corroding professional instincts of what's right. Hospitals are a slow-motion zone of forms and caution. How much is useful, and how much is wasteful? No one knows. End-of-life care is a zone of paranoia, where some nursing homes send ninety-year-olds in their last days to intensive care units to be poked with needles and die listening to the alarms of beeping medical machinery, instead of peacefully in the company of loved ones. But nursing homes can't be blamed if Grandpa dies on someone else's watch.

Law has become an invisible shield between doctor and patient. The most mundane visits are affected. A pediatrician friend in Charlotte, North Carolina, described to me how his good judgment has been undermined by the need to justify his decisions. "I used to see a healthy child and write a couple of lines on the patient chart. Now I write twenty or thirty lines, detailing everything I see that indicates the child is normal. Does this make sense? No, it's counterproductive to someone who actually needs to go back through the charts at some point. I'm also less open and spontaneous, particularly with patients I don't know well. I don't like feeling this way, and it takes some of the joy out of practice, but I feel I need to protect myself."

People who are sick need empathy, and hope. They need to trust their doctors, not feel doctors are protecting themselves. When tragedy occurs, or mistakes happen, patients need honesty, not stonewalling. Instead, when errors are made, doctors don't admit them, or apologize, for fear of exacerbating liability. One mother whose son had died in routine surgery at Mass General called me in frustration because she couldn't get anyone there to talk with her about what had happened. "Do I have to sue," she asked, "just to learn the truth?"

I had minor knee surgery a couple of years ago, opening a small personal window into our health care culture. The sea of forms and waivers was astounding. Does anyone ever read them? Another requirement was to have a preoperative examination. I'm sure that makes sense in many situations, but mine was a forty-five-minute procedure using local anesthesia, the knee equivalent of having dental work. When I asked what was involved in this preoperative examination, I learned that it was the full megillah of blood work, X-rays, electrocardiograms—more than $1,000 worth. It so happened that I had all those tests just the month before in my annual checkup. I offered to send over the results, saving my insurer the money and saving me the harmful zaps from the X-ray. No, the hospital said: no preop, no surgery. I offered to sign a formal waiver releasing the hospital from any liability from my failure to update my physical. But the hospital didn't trust justice to honor a waiver by a consenting adult. It was hopeless.

Restoring health to American health care requires many changes in order to better deliver services and align incentives; many of these choices involve allocating expensive resources, such as MRIs, to situations where they are most needed. None of those choices will be made sensibly, at least not systemwide, until there is a system of justice that doctors trust to defend their reasonable judgments.

RETHINKING THE CIVIL JURY

Like the rest of us, judges have witnessed this expansion of legal exposure, and many don't like it. But they feel powerless to do anything. Making a legal ruling based on the broader social effects of a lawsuit—say, whether charities are liable for their volunteers' driving—is inconceivable to most judges. Judges will sometimes reduce an absurd amount of damages (though not the $17 million verdict against the Catholic Archdiocese in Milwaukee), but almost never limit the claim in advance. A few years ago, when debating the judge in the McDonald's hot-coffee case, I suggested that the reasonableness of selling hot coffee from a takeout window should be decided as a matter of law. His response perfectly captured current judicial orthodoxy: "Who am I to judge?"

Judicial deference is ingrained so deeply that most judges can't conceive of having the power to keep claims reasonable. Even a whisper in the direction, they know, will elicit an explosion from the trial lawyers: *You're taking away the right to sue.* Judges, lawyers, even tort reformers, shrivel up at this point—it's like being accused of stealing. The charge itself is enough to end the discussion.

The rhetoric about "the right to sue" is itself misleading, just another example of how the trial lawyers ply their trade. Access to courts is indeed a core value. The courthouse door should never be barred, even for frivolous claims. After all, somebody has to decide what's frivolous. But who decides? When leaning on their

horn about "the right to sue," the trial lawyers are deliberately con-
fusing the concept of universal access to the court (which no one
threatens), with a presumption that the jury always decides who
wins and who loses. The choice, they tell us, is between the jury
or a stacked deck. "I trust the jury system and I trust the American people and their common sense," as billionaire trial lawyer
Richard Scruggs put it, "far more than the National Association of
Manufacturers to protect the American public."

Last I looked, judges' salaries aren't paid by the National Association of Manufacturers, although the financing of judicial elections has become pretty unseemly. Scruggs himself has pleaded
guilty to trying to bribe a judge. But the need to restore respect
to the state judicial selection process does not reduce the need to
reestablish the rule of law. When it comes to deciding who sets
boundaries, judge or jury, America doesn't have a choice—juries
can't draw legal boundaries. Judges must take this responsibility,
or else there's no one in the courtroom doing that job.

Excuse me, the retort comes, what about the Constitution?
Doesn't the Constitution require juries to decide who wins?
Actually no, at least not if the lawsuit turns on a conclusion that
should be decided as a matter of law. Society needs to know, for
example, whether a seesaw is a reasonable risk. That requires
a legal ruling by the judge. Criminal cases are different. Under
the Sixth Amendment only the jury can convict you of a crime.
The jury is our protection against power-crazed prosecutors. But
for private lawsuits (known as civil cases), the Seventh Amendment explicitly incorporates common law practice, which divides
the responsibility between judge and jury. Juries decide disputed
facts—who is telling the truth, say, or who ran the red light.
Judges interpret and apply the law—deciding which are valid
claims as a matter of law.

The language of the Seventh Amendment is hardly a model of
clarity: "In suits at common law . . . , the right of trial by jury shall
be preserved, and no fact tried by a jury, shall be otherwise re-

examined . . . , than according to the rules of the common law." But the division of responsibility between judges deciding law and juries deciding facts is well settled, at least in theory. In the debates over ratification of the Constitution, the future chief justice John Marshall stated categorically: "What is the object of a jury trial? To inform the Court of the facts."

Judges today give lip service to the distinction between fact and law, but as one scholar put it, there's "a strong tendency to let all issues go to the jury without discriminating among them." Letting the jury decide is easy; it "reduces judicial effort and the risk of reversal." For most of our legal history this practice had no obvious impact on public trust. Prior to the 1960s judges didn't need to keep tight reins on hot-coffee claims or $54 million suits over lost pants. There weren't any claims like these.

In the 1960s legal theorists reconceived civil justice to be a neutral process. In what became known as "the neutral process movement," judges should not only be impartial, but should avoid asserting values of right and wrong altogether. Who knows what bias lurks in the heart of the judge? Appellate courts admonished judges not to dismiss any claim unless "it appears beyond doubt that the plaintiff can prove no set of facts in support of his claim which would entitle him to recover." Since most cases involve applying standards of reasonableness to the facts at hand—what are known as mixed questions of law and fact—it is easy to pass the buck to the jury.

At first slowly, then more rapidly, the word got out that you could argue almost anything in these "neutral process" courts. In the early 1970s a $1 million verdict made the headlines: Someone got rich from an accident! Today it would have to be $100 million to get noticed. Trial lawyers, congregating at the intersection of human tragedy and human greed, have convinced the public that any tragedy is a reason to get rich. The average size of jury verdicts in accident cases doubled from 1996 to 2003—to more than $1.2 million.

I can see the brickbats coming my way: "The Constitution gives us the right to trial by jury. You're taking away our rights. Suing for anything is part of what it means to live in a free country."

Let's go back to first principles. The rights our founders gave us are rights against state power. "Congress shall make no law . . . abridging freedom of speech." "The right of the people to be secure in their persons, houses, papers, and effects . . . shall not be violated." "No person shall be deprived of life, liberty, or property, without due process of law." The Constitution guarantees our freedom mainly by protecting us against coercive state power.

A private lawsuit, by contrast, is a use of the state's coercive power against another private party. It's just like indicting someone; it's just an indictment for money. But lawsuits don't have the safeguards that apply to prosecutors—no grand jury, no clearly defined criminal statutes. We would never tolerate a prosecutor bringing a baseless charge. Nor would we allow a prosecutor to threaten the death penalty for a misdemeanor. That would be a clear abuse of state power. Why, then, do we tolerate allowing self-interested private parties to invoke legal power unilaterally to threaten the livelihoods of other free citizens?

Letting anyone sue for almost anything does not honor our rights. It turns our rights upside down—law becomes the weapon of state power instead of our protection against state power. Worse, unlike a criminal prosecution, state power is being used for personal gain. People like the lost-pants man get it in their heads that getting rich at the expense of someone else is somehow virtuous. Trial lawyers pretend that they're Robin Hood, with the modern twist that they keep much of the money for themselves. This modern approach to lawsuits is not about justice—it's about greed in the clothing of justice.

Justice is certainly available today for valid grievances—this is a good thing, which must be preserved. But even those remedies are impaired by the hands-off judicial attitude that tolerates nearly endless foot-dragging by guilty defendants. Modern justice is also

available, however, for extortion. That's the source of the legal fear
that undermines our freedom. That's why legislatures and judges
must draw legal boundaries.

TAKING BACK CONTROL OF THE COURTROOM

In 2002 Federal Judge Janis Jack, in Corpus Christi, Texas, found
herself presiding over almost 10,000 claims on behalf of alleged
victims of silicosis. Silicosis is a terrible disease, caused by intense
exposure to airborne particles of sand and rock. Slivers of quartz
lodge in the lungs and cause slow suffocation. In what is known
as the "Hawk's Nest incident," nearly 600 workers died of silicosis
after drilling through almost pure silica as part of a Tennessee Val-
ley Authority project in the 1930s. The symptoms of silicosis are
similar to those of asbestosis, except that the X-ray profile is very
different, with small, rounded opacities in the upper or middle
zones of the lung instead of irregular linear opacities at the base
and periphery of the lung in cases of asbestosis. Silicosis is also far
rarer—causing about 2 percent as many deaths as from asbestos.
In the 1990s a group of lawyers who had represented asbestos
clients started bringing lawsuits on behalf of people who claimed
they had silicosis. Many of these cases were consolidated before
Judge Jack.

It would be impossible to try 10,000 cases in several lifetimes.
The usual course of these mass tort lawsuits is that a few cases get
tried, and then the rest settle. Judges basically see their role as ref-
erees, and look forward to the day when all the paperwork ends.
Judge Jack did something almost unique in the annals of modern
litigation. She took it upon herself to investigate the underlying
validity of the claims. Judge Jack spent more than a year research-
ing the science of silicosis and reviewing the actual files of the
claimants.

What Judge Jack found was that the claims were a sham. The
litigation had basically been mass-produced by lawyers who adver-

tised for potential plaintiffs, invited them to a mobile X-ray truck, and then paid doctors to sign their names on preprinted diagnoses. The details of the fraud, laid out in Judge Jack's 250-page opinion, were shocking: One doctor, responsible for more than 1,200 plaintiffs' diagnoses, made all his diagnostic evaluations in less than seventy-two hours. Two-thirds of the claimants had previously filed asbestos claims, surprising in that it would be a clinical rarity for a patient to have both silicosis and asbestosis.

What shocked the legal community, however, were not the details of this scheme—anyone associated with asbestos litigation has seen a similar scam in action for years, in which an estimated 90 percent of claims were bogus—but that a judge actually took the authority to declare that the emperor had no clothes. Until her decision, judges overseeing several hundred thousand cases had basically taken the position that the plaintiffs had the right to submit these bogus claims to the jury.

Judge Jack was emboldened by a 1993 decision by the Supreme Court, *Daubert v. Merrell Dow*, which holds that judges should rule on the validity of scientific experts; otherwise juries are swayed by "junk science." Judge Jack took *Daubert* one step farther and ruled on the validity of the claims themselves.

America needs a Judge Jack in every courtroom, not only reviewing science but drawing boundaries of reasonable risk and reasonable claims. Judges in America have never done that, at least not in personal injury law, because before the 1960s, as noted, there wasn't much of a need to. People didn't sue over a teacher grabbing hold of an unruly student, or over losing a pair of pants. Today social norms have been disrupted. No one knows what someone else may claim. Judges have to help restore order to this free-for-all.

But on what basis are judges supposed to decide? To most judges, the idea of looking inside themselves to decide what's reasonable is almost inconceivable. Judges are stuck in the rut of objective justification, avoiding any ruling they can't prove by external criteria.

NYU Professor Arthur Miller, criticizing use of summary rulings by judges, is horrified at the notion of "result-oriented" decisions that, in the name of legal policy, might draw on the judge's own values: "Judges are human, and their personal sense of whether a plaintiff's claim seems 'implausible' can subconsciously infiltrate even the most careful analysis." Professor Miller basically has it backward. Judges are *supposed* to get rid of claims that seem implausible. The core assumption of modern orthodoxy—that judges should avoid value judgments—is what keeps justice from being trustworthy.

Judges must affirmatively protect reasonable social norms of right and wrong. In the $54 million lost-pants lawsuit, the judge should have called in the parties and said something like: "Maybe you have a claim for a few hundred dollars in small claims court, but you have no right to use justice as a tool of extortion. Case dismissed, without prejudice to refiling elsewhere with an appropriate claim." But the judge thought his role was just to preside over a neutral process, at one point saying he "didn't want to belittle the case." And so the lives of the Korean immigrants were turned upside down because, in the name of neutrality, the judge refused to do what everyone knew was right.

People go through the day relying on their reasonable instincts. They *sense* right and wrong, as they do with most criminal prohibitions. That same generalized understanding of right and wrong must hold true for all social interaction: how teachers deal with students, doctors with patients, supervisors with employees, and dry cleaners with their customers.

If justice is just a neutral process—with no effort by judges to rein in extreme claims or dubious defenses—then people know they can't rely on their instincts of what's reasonable. They become self-conscious and defensive in daily dealings. For them to feel free in daily interactions, legal boundaries must correspond with their reasonable sense of right and wrong. That requires judges to apply social norms when drawing boundaries of reasonable claims. "The first requirement of a sound body of law," Justice Oliver Wendell

Holmes, Jr., wrote, "is that it should correspond with the actual feelings and demands of the community."

Judges must constantly draw on their values, acting as surrogates for society for what constitute reasonable claims. It is correct that a judge can never "eliminate altogether the personal measure of the interpreter," as Justice Cardozo observed, but he went on to explain that society can't function without a ruling by someone:

> You may say there is no assurance that judges will interpret the *mores* of their day more wisely and truly than other men. I am not disposed to deny this, but in my view it is quite beside the point. The point is rather that this power of interpretation must be lodged somewhere. . . .

The judge's rulings are not supposed to be based on personal preferences. It's "not what I believe to be right," Justice Cardozo noted. "It is what I may reasonably believe that some other man of normal intellect and conscience might reasonably look upon as right."

Many judges have argued to me that this is the job of legislatures. But hundreds of legislators can't crowd into the courtroom in each case. Law is too complex to write a rule for every situation. Legal principles that guide social behavior are unavoidably general—for example, whether someone acted reasonably in the circumstances. Judges in the particular case must apply social norms to give meaning to those legal principles—for example, whether it is reasonable for citizens to bear the risk of playground accidents. The former president of the Israeli Supreme Court Aharon Barak refers to this role of the judge as "creat[ing] law within the framework of the law."

I can feel the next objection practically bursting out of many of you. What about judicial activism? Conservatives have railed for years against the activist judges. Indeed, at the same time judges were letting claimants sue for almost anything, they were taking control of prisons and causing riots when they ordered children bussed to different neighborhoods. These judges felt just fine making rulings as a matter of law that effectively preempted the legislature. The judge gallops off on a white charger to fix the ills of society but in private disputes sits on his hands, letting people in his courtroom argue anything. How can we come to terms with this Jekyll and Hyde performance?

This schizophrenic judicial behavior reflects the philosophy of the 1960s, a preoccupation with the plight of the individual. While the judge trusts himself to interfere with democratic institutions on behalf of the individual, the same judge doesn't trust himself to choose among competing individuals in the courtroom. Who is he to judge? The common thread is an active antagonism to authority. The school board isn't doing a good job educating the students? The judge teams up with the plaintiff to take over the schools. Someone feels aggrieved? The judge lets the plaintiff sue for the moon. Leaning over backward for the alleged victim is the common thread in this otherwise inconsistent judicial philosophy.

The result, ironically, has been to victimize the entire society. Our institutions are immobilized by the competing demands. What about my rights? What about *my* rights? What about MY rights? The growing cacophony, we see every day, demonstrates the growing misalignment of justice from the society around it.

Giving judges the responsibility of drawing boundaries of risks and rights is unavoidable. Only a judge—a human present in the courtroom—can make the distinctions based on particular context. The small-town doctor handling an emergency should be held to a different standard than a brain surgeon in New York. A teacher understands that he can't haul off and slug a student. But the teacher also must be able to restrain a disruptive student without fear of a legal claim. Judges can draw these lines, consistent with past decisions. Juries can't, because they're not accountable for consistency. Statutes can't, because they're not able to evaluate the context. Judges must take responsibility to maintain the boundaries of what's reasonable in the courtroom.

RESTORING LAW TO LAWSUITS

The block party in Bayonne, New Jersey, was a friendly, crowded affair, with kids running around and parents shooting the breeze. Then the accident occurred. A five-year-old riding around on his bicycle with training wheels bumped into a one-year-old, knocking her to the ground and sending her off to get some stitches. Next came the lawsuit: The parents of the one-year-old sued the parents of the five-year-old for not exercising better supervision. The case made its way up to the New Jersey Supreme Court, which ordered the claim to be dismissed. The law doesn't require parents in these settings to defend against "honest errors." Otherwise, the court observed, people might stop holding block parties. This case illustrates the first of three major changes needed to restore trust to justice.

  1. *Judges must draw boundaries of reasonableness as a matter of law.* Giving judges the job of drawing legal boundaries is not a hard concept, at least in theory. The difficulty of this task is that after several decades of open floodgates, the boundaries have been washed away. Where would we start? One litmus test for interjecting a ruling of law is where a claim or defense might undermine reasonable activities of people not in the courtroom. If allowing a claim might result in lakes closing down, or playgrounds being stripped of fun equipment, or volunteers being barred from charities, then the judge should make a legal ruling defining the boundaries of such claims.

  Deciding where to draw the lines is more difficult. Most judges would be happy to draw these boundaries as long as they could find the answer in a lawbook. Unfortunately, there is no book that says what's reasonable in the circumstances. Moreover, social norms have become muddled as a result of the legal free-for-all in the last few decades. As suggested earlier, risk commissions are needed to establish norms in areas of confusion, such as children's play. One thing judges can do immediately is stop abusive and extreme claims, such as the $54 million lawsuit by the lost-pants man. Just knowing that judges see their job as keeping claims and defenses reasonable will be an important boost to our daily freedom. For the first time in our lives, justice will be committed to setting boundaries of reasonable dispute.

Legislatures could also help and would revolutionize the courtroom by enacting a simple statute along these lines:

> Judges shall take the responsibility to draw the boundaries of
> reasonable dispute as a matter of law, applying common law
> principles and statutory guidelines. In making these rulings,
> judges shall consider the potential effects of claims on society
> at large.

Britain in 2006 passed a law explicitly authorizing judges to consider whether allowing a claim might "discourage . . . a desirable activity." This kind of legislative leadership is unlikely in most American states, at least for the time being. Probably the right order of change is a few pointed appellate decisions—please, judges, start drawing boundaries—followed by statutes that explicitly give judges this responsibility.

  2. *Judges must actively manage the conduct of each case.* The most rudimentary requirements of fair justice—keeping cases on a reasonable time frame, making judgments about how much discovery is needed—require value judgments by the judge. Litigants shouldn't have to endure a legal gauntlet for years to see if a claim or defense is valid. Judges must constantly draw boundaries—not only on ultimate issues in the case but in getting the case to speedy

resolution. Trust in justice is impossible without constant application of legal values. This is how it works in other countries; in Germany, for example, judges call in parties at the outset of a case and
spend hours working through issues to limit the scope of claims
and defenses so that the case can get to a fair resolution quickly.

3. *Establish special courts for areas requiring special expertise.*
Some areas of society are too far gone; distrust and insecurity have
become imbued in the culture and are unlikely to be dislodged
with any incremental reform. In these situations what's required
is a clean break: establishing a special court dedicated to predict-
able rulings on standards of behavior. America has a long tradition
of special courts in areas needing specific expertise—admiralty
courts, tax courts, family courts, and bankruptcy courts, for example. There are scores of administrative tribunals, in areas ranging
from Social Security to vaccine liability. The workers' compensation system was put in place one hundred years ago to replace slow
and erratic justice for workplace accidents.

A special court is needed in America for medical malpractice
claims. I'll go further. It is virtually impossible to make the choices
needed to bring order to American health care without a system
of justice that can reliably uphold standards of care. Setting standards is not the problem—there are established standard-setting
bodies. What's missing is a court that is trusted to uphold those
standards.

A broad coalition—including large consumer groups such as
AARP, patient safety organizations, public health experts, as well as
doctors, hospitals, and other providers—has come together behind
doing pilots of an administrative court with the following characteristics: judges dedicated to health care claims; written judicial
opinions applying standards of care rather than jury verdicts; neutral experts rather than hired guns; expedited proceedings with
incentives for early settlements; payments of noneconomic dam-

ages based on a schedule for different injuries; and mechanisms to compile data to learn from mistakes.

An expert health court would likely pay more people, with lower average awards and dramatically lower legal expenses. The most important role of a special health court, however, is to provide a solid legal foundation for overhauling American health care. A court that is trusted to defend reasonable medical judgments can begin to thaw the legal chill that now impedes daily professional interaction. New guidelines to minimize wasteful regional variations in care, and to encourage humane end-of-life care, can be established and enforced. Bureaucrats can rethink whether all the paperwork is really needed; much of it is aimed at self-protection. Maybe doctors will start being empathic again.

Aligning the incentives of providers with good social policy cannot be accomplished as long as doctors are focused mainly on self-protection. That's why special health courts should be created to provide a platform of reliability. Health care can't be fixed without it.

For many, the hardest part of giving judges boundary-setting responsibility is that we don't trust them. It is inevitable that judges will make a certain number of bad rulings. But at least the rulings will be in writing for all to see and can be appealed to a higher court and, if really stupid, overturned by statute passed by the legislature. But having no rulings—letting all claims, however unreasonable, go to the jury—is like having a perfect record of bad rulings. In the current system, people see legal danger in the most ordinary encounters and go through the day acting as if they might be liable, thinking: Why take the risk?

Restoring the responsibility to judges and legislatures to draw the boundaries of claims is a major doctrinal change, almost comparable in scope to the shifts that occurred in the 1960s. But we don't really have a choice. Those boundaries are essential to the rule of law. Our freedom to make sense of daily choices depends on them. Sooner or later, as former Harvard president and law dean Derek Bok observed, "our legal system [must] empower someone to keep watch and make sure that the process as a whole is meeting the needs of those whom it purportedly serves."

CHAPTER 5

BUREAUCRACY CAN'T TEACH

TEAM Academy, a public charter school in Newark, New Jersey, started in 2002, has a record that most educators only dream about. Recruiting students from the worst projects in Newark, without any academic requirements, it has become one of the most successful schools in the state. The opening class of fifth graders initially tested at the 21st percentile in reading comprehension. One year later they were at the 55th percentile. In math the improvement was from the 31st to the 91st percentile.

"We don't actually worry much about improving scores," the founding principal Ryan Hill noted. "We spend our time building the culture. We work hard teaching the students the importance of respect for others and self-respect. If the school culture is good, the scores take care of themselves."

Culture is by far the most important indicator of success of a school. Within minutes of walking into a school, educators say, they can tell whether it is successful. They can feel the culture. The culture is reflected in the interactions among students, teachers, principals, and parents—in the manners, in the energy, in the humor, in the respect afforded others, in the self-restraint, in their aspirations, in school pride.

Good school cultures are also reflected in what is absent. It would be hard to find a successful school where law and bureaucracy were even noticeable. Teachers and principals in good school cultures are focused not on bureaucratic compliance but on doing what makes sense to them. As they go through the day, they feel free to act on their instincts of how best to deal with a student or situation. This freedom requires a legal structure—a structure that affirmatively protects the authority of teachers and principals to make choices that reflect their values of what a good school should be.

That's what a culture is—a framework of shared values. TEAM Academy is part of a network of charter schools called KIPP (Knowledge Is Power Program). KIPP has very definite values. Its motto is prominently posted: "Work Hard. Be Nice." Working hard is what everyone does. TEAM has classes until 5 p.m. every weekday, two hours longer than most public schools. TEAM also has a half day of classes on Saturdays, unheard of in public schools. The "Be Nice" part of the slogan is not wishful thinking but an active program to put each student on a personal journey toward self-respect. KIPP teaches a six-stage moral development program, in which the lowest scale of motivation is the desire to avoid punishment, and the highest is making choices simply because it's the right thing to do.

The positive energy at TEAM Academy is palpable. Not having to worry about baseline concerns—safety, politeness—liberates everyone to be more open and productive. When I was visiting, students came up to the principal easily, saying hi, or making a joke, or asking about some upcoming program. Students also came up to me, extended their hands, and asked how I was enjoying the visit. In the classroom all eyes were on the teacher. There was often humor even in the mistakes. The student sent out of classroom for talking during class was introduced as "the-boy-who-can't-help-himself." He smiled, and sat down in the office and read a book.

Culture is deceptively powerful because it operates mainly in undercurrents of social interaction that are felt rather than explicitly asserted. You can tell a lot just in the way people talk with each other. Culture is its own authority. Like a strong tide, the culture pushes people toward behaving in a certain way. Good school cultures bring out the best in both teachers and students.

No healthy culture can be built or maintained unless its values are enforced. That's why accountability is one of the core values at TEAM Academy—with definite consequences for destructive conduct. "We have some wonderful, nice kids who don't get their homework done consistently," observed Heidi Moore, a teacher at TEAM. "We have to hold them hostage to have them get it done. . . . Our kids have spent K to 4 [kindergarten to fourth grade] in schools with no homework and no accountability. If you asked them, 'How many of you used to get in fights at your old school?' ninety-five percent of them would raise their hands. . . . These are twelve-year-old kids who have faced no consequences throughout their lives."

The mechanisms of accountability at TEAM are clear and taught in the first few weeks of school. The school has what it calls "paychecks," which act as a kind of interim report card on citizenship and diligence, with certain benefits for high marks, such as takeout pizza on Fridays or an occasional field trip. Students who fail to meet certain broad standards—"not yet at the level of respect and character and work ethic they need to be successful in life"—are not allowed to go on the end-of-year trip to places like Washington and Utah. "We talk about the choices they're making all the time," Ms. Moore observed. "No one is surprised when they earn or don't earn. I had one student come up to me and say, 'Ms. Moore, why didn't I get a ticket to Utah?' I said, 'Because every time you make a bad choice—' And she cut me off: 'I get really disrespectful.' So they know!"

A good school culture itself teaches students the most important life lesson: how to participate in society. We tend to shrink away from the idea of "imposing" values, but the father of sociology, Emile Durkheim, considered socialization of youth at least as important a goal for schools as reading and arithmetic. Schools are settings, sociologist Richard Arum observes, "where children learn socially appropriate behavior, values and interpersonal skill from teachers, principals and fellow students." "All through life, you need codes of behavior in order to get along in whatever you do," observes Professor William Damon, a leading expert on adolescence. "You need to be respectful and honest, you need to have integrity and character, whether you end up driving a truck or being a doctor."

Reformers don't focus on school culture. Cultures are too complex, without objective metrics. To our modern sensibility, the idea of building a culture seems both presumptuous (whose values are being asserted?) and futile. A culture, many seem to believe, grows by forces beyond human control. In an enterprise of manageable size, however, cultures are man-made. Like a garden, the culture of a school or office is planted and maintained by deliberate assertion of values by the people in charge.

In a study of good high schools in the 1980s, Sara Lightfoot found that the cultures of private and parochial schools evolved over generations. Successful "turnaround" public schools, by contrast, were built through the force of personality of the individual principal. All these cultures share a trait, however, that transcends differences in school history, values, and goals. In every successful school, teachers and principals feel free to act on their best judgment. All day long in the classroom they own their choices. This freedom allows full expression of the teacher's personality and enthusiasm. It allows nuanced judgments of the conflicts and failures through the day.

Values don't come to life without the freedom to assert them. Enthusiasm energizes the entire culture—"There's nothing so contagious," the saying goes, "as enthusiasm." There's no enthusiasm, however, without spontaneity and originality. That's how people develop a sense of ownership of the culture. At TEAM Academy the teachers and principal all get together to decide what they want the students to learn, and then the teachers figure out for themselves how to do it. In almost every classroom the teacher arranged the desks differently—some in rows, some in communal tables, some in a U within a U, some pulling up chairs in a corner for readings together. "Letting the teachers decide for themselves how to teach, even what books to use, means they can innovate," Hill noted. "When they invent the program, they're invested in it. It's also more interesting for students." The need for teachers and principals to feel ownership of their daily choices is usually overlooked because, I suppose, we take it for granted. Yet no school succeeds without it. If values breathe life into a culture, the constant choices by teachers and principals are how this oxygen gets made.

Building a good culture is a challenge. But it must be the goal. When there's a good culture, all challenges are like coasting downhill. Without a good school culture, no matter how much money is spent, every day is a struggle. TEAM Academy had the advantage of starting fresh, with an uncompromising assertion of core values at the outset. But the building block of good school cultures is the same everywhere: it is the freedom of teachers and principals, all day long, to make sense of the situations before them. In most American public schools, that freedom has been smothered by ever-thickening layers of bureaucracy and legal rights.

THE BUREAUCRATIC SCHOOL

"Most people in the real world probably can't imagine how bureaucratic schools have become," one former teacher from the Bronx explained. The advent of "high-stakes testing has created its own special level of weirdness" as if the school were in "some sort of lockdown." "To prevent cheating, all words and letters posted around the classroom—even student names—had to be covered up. So the walls were taped up with newspapers. . . . Teachers are not allowed to grade papers or do anything productive during the test—instead we were forced to circle the classroom to prevent cheating. But we couldn't look at the students because that might scare them. . . . Meanwhile the rest of the school is frozen in place. Other classes not taking the test had to sit in one room, without instruction or other activity that might make disturbing noises. . . . Proctors walk around like police to make sure no one is violating any of these rules."

School reformers for decades have tried different ideas and techniques to try to make schools work better. The last major effort is the No Child Left Behind Law, passed by Congress in 2001 to mandate nationwide testing and impose penalties if schools don't meet certain goals. Most reforms have salutary goals. But none of it seems to have done much good. Five years after No Child Left Behind went into effect, reading scores for fourth graders had increased modestly, while scores for eighth grade declined slightly. Overall, reading scores in elementary and high schools have stayed flat for almost forty years. In that period the ranking of American students has consistently fallen relative to their peers in other developed countries.

All these reforms have been based on an unspoken assumption: that better organization is the key to fixing whatever ails schools. The theory is that by imposing more organizational requirements— better teacher credentials, more legal rights, detailed curricula, the pressure of tests—schools will get better. That's the theory. The effect, however, is to remove the freedom needed to succeed at any aspect of teachers' responsibilities—how they teach, how they relate to students, and how they coordinate their goals with administrators. The extent and effects of bureaucracy may indeed surprise people from the real world. Here are some snapshots.

BUREAUCRACY LEVEL ONE: SMOTHERING THE TEACHER

In 2006 a group of teachers in New York kept diaries that chronicled how they made it through the day. The smallest details of classroom life were governed by rules. There were rules on how teachers organized themselves and rules on how to present materials: "Sometimes I feel like I'm a robot regurgitating the scripted dialogue." The rules even dictated how teachers responded to students—for example, forbidding a teacher from calling on students who raised their hands during the first part of class. One teacher's diary contained this entry: "Teach mini-lesson. Read aloud book by author we have selected. Student raises hand with question. Tell him to put hand down. Students not allowed to ask questions during mini-lesson. Feel guilty."

Almost no act, no matter how innocent, was free of bureaucratic constraint. A mother of a third grader arrived with a supply of birthday cupcakes but was sent away. There was a rule against parents in the classroom.

How many rules are there in American schools? The people in charge don't know. As far as I can tell, no one with responsibility—not Congress, not any board of education—has ever even tried to catalog all the rules and rights that govern our schools. They just assume that rules are the way to do things properly; the more rules the better. In 2004 Common Good did an inventory of all the legal rules imposed on a high school in New York City. It found thousands of discrete legal requirements, imposed by every level of government. There was no act or decision—how to be fair, how to provide feedback, how to arrange the classroom, how to clean a window, how to keep files, how to order copier paper—that wasn't covered by a rule.

Teachers, like most people, hate bureaucracy. A 2007 California study on teacher retention, trying to understand why 18,000 teachers quit each year, found that bureaucracy was the leading factor. "There is no rhyme or reason for many things we are asked to do," said a teacher in California who quit after eight years because of the "wasted time and energy" caused by "many silly procedures," such as a "lengthy request process for routine maintenance such as repairing an overhead light in a classroom."

Forms are everywhere. Most schools require teachers to write up detailed course plans for each week, knowing full well that no one ever reads them. "The paperwork overload is out of control," observed one special education teacher. She went on to describe some of the requirements: "I spend at least 4 hours testing every child, 2 hours writing every IEP [individualized education plan, required by federal law], at least 5 hours testing for triennial reviews, and another 2–3 hours writing the report for EVERY child. Most of this takes place on weekends or after school gets out. . . . Teachers are burning out." In Alabama, two thousand teachers went on strike in 2004 because of the wasted time spent on forms. "Teachers will spend six hours a day in the classroom," an Alabama teachers' union official said, "and then go home and spend three, four, or five hours a night filling out paperwork."

There are only so many hours in the day, and bureaucracy would be evil enough if all it did was divert teacher energy. But rules also dictate choices that make no sense. "I have kids who are supposed to learn 7th grade history, but they read at a second-grade level," a teacher in California observed. "We should be allowed to figure out how to deal with those kinds of problems, . . . [not] required to use curriculum materials that don't address those students' needs." Debbie Sherlock, an elementary school teacher in Queens, New York, echoed this frustration: "Your hands are tied; you know kids cannot learn this way, but this is what you have to do."

It is impossible to get away from bureaucracy. Loudspeakers blare out announcements such as "Teachers, the faculty meeting will begin at 3:30"; "Ms. Jackson, please report to room 214"; "tickets to the football game will be sold at the gym after three o'clock." In one day, an observer in a class in New York City counted sixteen interruptions by the school loudspeaker. At one point the teacher was ordered to immediately collect the students' reading books and turn them in, causing a twenty-five-minute gap in teaching. Like a sort of shock torture, the announcements seem designed to destroy the concentration of teacher and students on the subject at hand. "I feel as if I teach between the interruptions," one thirty-year veteran in California observed.

No one would ever design a system that is so intrusive. Once the idea of management by rule takes root, however, it grows like kudzu. The rule against parents in the classroom was probably prompted by some angry father who made a nuisance of himself. Most principals can distinguish between an angry father and one bringing birthday cupcakes, but rules can't—except, of course, with more rules. "I can't even go back and observe at my old public school." Ryan Hill observed. "It's too exhausting, watching the teacher try to follow all the rules. Even the smallest choice is a struggle. It's as if the teacher is tied in knots, struggling to get out."

To many teachers, No Child Left Behind is the last straw. Teachers generally support standardized testing, but the obsessive pursuit of scores to the exclusion of all else, teachers believe, has become another bureaucratic rigidity. Claire Pulignano, a teacher in Florida, tells what happened to an English class where the students were reading *To Kill a Mockingbird*. "The principal then came into a meeting and made real clear that the emphasis was to be on [the standardized test], and we could pretty much forget what had been in the curriculum. More and more we're told, 'You will teach this and this on this day.' I love teaching, I love kids, but it's become harder and harder when you're teaching to the test. *Can you hear the discouragement in my voice?*"

Demoralization has never been considered a way to run a successful organization, but demoralization is the status quo at many, perhaps most, schools in America.

BUREAUCRACY LEVEL TWO: DISRUPTIVE STUDENTS FILL THE VACUUM

Legalistic organization has undermined the moral authority needed to maintain order and an environment conducive to learning. Every day, in schools across the country, students wander around the classroom, disrupting the class and confronting teachers with an in-your-face attitude. In many schools, disruption is the norm. Nick Bagley, who was an eighth-grade teacher in the Bronx, described a "pervasive atmosphere of not respecting authority. There was very little that was outside the pale. Pretty much anything went. Cursing, screaming, yelling, leaving the room, pounding on the door." A report on Philadelphia schools in 2007 by Ellen Green-Ceisler describes classrooms where "little or no learning was actually occurring" and "many of the students in attendance were listening to headphones, sleeping, doodling or wandering around the room talking or shouting." In a 2001 Public Agenda survey, 43 percent of high school teachers said they spent more time maintaining order than teaching.

No enterprise, no society, can succeed where disorder is the norm. This point, generally identified with Thomas Hobbes, is as apt for schools as for a seventeenth-century society wracked by civil war. Disruptive behavior by one student effectively destroys the ability of the other twenty-nine students to focus on the lesson at hand. Learning is impossible—even the best teacher can't compete with the disruptive student.

Violence is not unusual. One in seven teachers in urban schools, one study found, had been physically assaulted by his students. In 2007 in Philadelphia a sixty-year-old teacher had his neck broken when he attempted to confiscate an iPod—while thirty students watched. In the same month another Philadelphia teacher suffered a concussion and a broken jaw when he was hit by a student as he tried to calm a disruptive class. The same teacher had been sprayed with a fire extinguisher twice in the weeks before. Joe Smith, an eighth-grade math teacher, after trying to stop a student from making phone calls during class, was hit repeatedly with the phone and a dictionary and choked with his necktie. "I could have died," the teacher said. The teacher was especially bitter about the double standard: "If I hit that student, the police would have been there in three seconds. She hit me, it took them an hour and a half. We have no protection."

Physical assault has to be major before principals will bother to try to discipline a student. A teacher in the Bronx tells of two girls who got in a violent fight during class—the punishment was that each had to fill out a form giving her version of the story, after which they returned to class. Another teacher in New York tells this story: "There was a teacher here, the best teacher here, she was punched in the face. The kid was sent to the dean, and he said, 'I don't want to deal with this,' and the kid was sent back to her class—to her class!"

The decline in order is worse in inner city schools, but hardly confined to them. One teacher from the suburbs told about a student from a well-to-do family who was misbehaving. As the teacher tried to get him to be quiet, the student walked up to the teacher in front of the entire class, put his hand over her mouth to stop her from talking, and then left the classroom for a few minutes before coming back. The teacher went straight to the principal, who just shrugged his shoulders and said there was nothing he could do. Only with persistence of the teacher, and the help of the union, did the student finally get suspended for two days.

There was probably no golden age of education, but fifty years ago most of these incidents would have been unthinkable. A survey of teachers in 1956 found that 95 percent reported that their students were either extremely well behaved or moderately well behaved. Today, by any definition, disorder is at epidemic levels. In most other developed countries, by contrast, student disorder is dealt with immediately or is barely a topic of discussion. We wonder why American students do so badly compared with foreign students.

Like all cultural phenomena, disorder in schools has many sources. But parochial schools and charter schools in inner-city neighborhoods do not have endemic disorder. There is one clear difference: Teachers in those schools have the authority to enforce values of common civility. In public schools, by contrast, discipline has been bureaucratized.

In New York City more than sixty steps and legal considerations are required to suspend a student for over five days. Denver is similar, with two levels of appeals. New York City's Legal Support Unit has a 210-page booklet, *Representing Students in Disciplinary Proceedings*. Just sending a disruptive student out of the classroom requires layers of bureaucratic compliance. A teacher must stop the class, call the security guard, fill out required forms, and allow the student "to present his/her version of the events." To suspend the student, the teacher must show up for multiple meetings with the parents and hearing officers—time now lost to her real job, which is to teach.

A legalistic regime on discipline, instead of supporting teacher authority, undermines it. Rules lay out teacher obligations, including, in New York City, an admonition against using any "language that tends to belittle" students. Instead of students feeling they must answer to the teacher, what they see, over and over, is that the teacher must answer to the form, or the rule, or the argument. Students understand the power of just making allegations. "Kids were very conscious of this," Eric Goldstein, the teacher in Rockland County, New York, observed. "It's difficult to do your job if you constantly have to worry about things you didn't do."

Most principals, overwhelmed by the process and the legal risks, have given up on trying to discipline students for obscenities, rudeness, interruptions, and even continued disruption. According to Eric Goldstein, "if you write something up and send it to the assistant principal, he'll send it right back and say, 'You deal with it.' " That seems to be standard operating procedure at most schools. A teacher in the Bronx described the kind of support most teachers get: "I carefully documented all the rude and disruptive behavior by one student, just like we were told to, and sent it to the administrators in a nice envelope. Then I waited two weeks—this student was interfering with the ability of everyone else to focus—and finally I got back a note saying, 'All of these behaviors are the sort that a teacher should be able to handle on her own.' "

Because students see teachers as largely powerless, they act accordingly. In the daily diaries kept by a small group of teachers in New York City in 2007 was an entry by a high school teacher about a student who called her "a fat ugly asshole" throughout the class period. A second-grade teacher described a student who was removed from the classroom for breaking crayons in half and throwing them at other students. When he returned to the class-room forty-five minutes later, "he had a plastic cup full of pretzels. Though I asked him to put them away he refused. He began smash-ing the pretzels on the table. . . . He then decided to throw the cup of pretzels around the room and began kicking the furniture."

Disorder is contagious, a kind of virus that takes over a school with only a few unchecked incidents. Young people aren't known for their maturity, and pushing the envelope becomes a sport. What's happened is a version of the broken windows thesis by sociologists James Q. Wilson and George L. Kelling. If broken win-dows in a building are not fixed, they suggest, "the tendency is for vandals to break a few more windows. Eventually, they . . . break into the building."

The windows of authority in American schools have been bro-ken now for decades. It's hard to pinpoint exactly when author-ity flipped. Probably the best case study is Gerald Grant's study of one high school in northern New York over two decades, *The World We Created at Hamilton High*. That high school had fallen into an abyss by the mid-1980s. But it's not hard to identify why the authority collapsed. The decline of order, as Professor Richard Arum details in *Judging School Discipline,* is directly tied to the rise of "due process."

Due process originally applied to schools in a case involving Viet-nam protests. Students do not "shed their constitutional rights," Justice Abe Fortas intoned, "at the schoolhouse gate." Due process, our constitutional protection against being sent to jail arbitrarily, now applied before a student could be sent home. Once the idea of due process was imported into schools, it was hard to draw the line. Courts overturned suspensions of school drug dealers on the basis that the accusations, though true, had not been grounded in adequate "probable cause."

Like a passing fad, the hyperdistrust by courts had largely dissipated by the end of the 1970s. Courts began cutting back on earlier opinions and suggested that the due process required was minimal in most cases. But the legal train had left the station. Everyone— students, parents, teachers, principals—now had the idea that daily choices had to be legally justified. Teachers came to believe, Gerald Grant found, that the rules existed to discipline them, not the students. Due process had become a governing idea of public schools. One legal aid organization had a thick manual just for due process rules, covering not only discipline but "matters related to grading, diploma denial, and other 'academic' decisions."

With due process came an explosion of bureaucracy. Schools can justify their disciplinary decisions if there's a clear rule against the conduct. One pernicious example is the idea of zero tolerance rules, invented in the 1980s to try to counteract the decline of school authority. With a clear rule, the theory went, a student who brought a weapon or drugs to school could summarily be sent home. The problem is that zero tolerance rules can't distinguish trivial from severe infractions. In 2001 a National Merit scholar at a high school in Fort Myers, Florida, was suspended because a small kitchen knife was found in the back seat of her car on school grounds (it had fallen out of a box when she was moving). One principal told of having to suspend a first-grade girl, because when the students were asked to bring in their favorite possessions, she brought the small penknife given to her by her grandfather. That'll teach her . . . what? That schools don't care about right and wrong?

Instead of bolstering school authority, zero tolerance rules have become a symbol of lack of authority to do what's right. " 'Zero tolerance' discipline policies that are enforced widely in U.S. schools are backfiring," was the headline that resulted from a 2006 report by the American Psychological Association (APA) on school discipline. According to Professor Cecil Reynolds, the head of the APA panel, "The 'one-size-fits-all' approach isn't working. Bringing aspirin to school is not the same as bringing cocaine. A plastic knife isn't the same as a handgun."

A legalistic approach to organizing schools, the Supreme Court thought, would promote fairness. Instead the legal mind-set has driven school culture onto the shoals of selfishness, not toward values of cooperation, mutual respect, and school pride. Moral authority has capsized. Teachers and principals find themselves doing whatever they can to hold on to the hull, while students amuse themselves scrambling around the slippery and disorganized deck.

BUREAUCRACY LEVEL THREE: MUTUAL SELF-DESTRUCTION

Bureaucracy, by substituting dictates and process for free choice, demoralizes teachers and gives resourceful adolescents the opportunity to destroy order. But it also does something else: It turns educators against each other. The worse schools have gotten, the more the different constituents—teachers' unions, principals' unions, custodial unions, boards of education—have sought to protect their prerogatives through legal mandates. Bureaucracy leads to mutual antipathy which leads to terminal bureaucracy.

The endless regulations imposed by the board of ed—for example, prohibiting teachers from calling on students during the minilesson—are equally matched by the rigid work rules imposed by the teachers' union. In New York City the teachers' union contract, 165 pages long, plus decades of accumulated arbitration rulings, dictates the hours worked (six hours twenty minutes), limits teacher duties, and restricts faculty conferences to a time that requires the principal to cancel classes. Until a "breakthrough" in the latest union contract, principals couldn't even put a critical comment in a teacher's file without official notice and the opportunity for a legal hearing.

Accountability for poor performance is nonexistent, as discussed shortly, except in a kind of black market. Effective principals can sometimes cajole or bully bad teachers into leaving but certainly don't have the management authority to do so. Some principals organize transfers of bad teachers to other schools in exchange for taking someone else's dregs, a phenomenon known as the "dance of the lemons." Some teachers in New York City end up in "rubber rooms," off-site holding pens for teachers who have no school assignments. They come, read books, or play video games—sometimes for years.

The bureaucratic stranglehold on principals extends to most of the basic tools of management. In New York they don't even have control over custodians, who have their own union contract. Eva Moskowitz, former chair of the New York City Council's education committee, wondered why paint crumbled at the top of walls in old schools. The reason, she discovered, was a union prohibition against painting walls higher than ten feet.

After decades of growing bureaucracy, disorder, and frustration, educators are at each other's throats. Instead of a culture of cooperation, the legalistic mind-set has bred a kind of anticulture in which educators use law as a weapon against each other. In 2004 the New York City Council held hearings on why nobody seemed able to make schools functional. The board of ed lawyer laid out in gory detail the "oppressive set of work rules" mandated by the union contract, and horror stories of terrible teachers impossible to terminate. The head of the teachers' union, Randi Weingarten, struck back in kind, citing hundreds of rules imposed by the board of education that try to make effective teaching into a form of legal compliance:

> every minute of the day and every inch of a classroom is dictated, the arrangement of desks, the format of the bulletin boards, the position in which Teachers should stand. . . . Teachers are demeaned, they are stripped of their profession-

alism, they are expected to behave like Robots and incapable of independent thought.

Like tired prizefighters staggering through the late rounds, the teachers, principals, and board of ed pummel each other with legal requirements. The only sure result is a TKO—a bureaucratic knockout of America's schools.

THE LIMITS OF ORGANIZATION

Organizing schools by legal bureaucracy is not, perhaps, America's finest innovation. Standardized protocols and lessons, the theory goes, would make schools as efficient as factories. But rules and rights just kept piling up, decade after decade, with no serious effort at making sense of them. The idea was to eliminate human error by, in effect, eliminating human choice. But even Soviet central planners wouldn't tolerate a system that barred nature hikes, or prevented teachers from calling on students who raised their hands, or let students run wild in the classroom.

Rolling up our sleeves to reorganize this legal tangle would be a mistake, however. There are too many rules, and they are too interconnected. Organization is the problem, not the solution. Choices can't be programmed without destroying the human skills needed to run a school.

The efficacy of organizational systems, industrial psychologists tell us, varies dramatically with the activity. At one end of the spectrum are assembly lines, artificial closed environments designed for standard inputs and standard products. On the other end are uniquely personal endeavors, such as the arts; trying to put those uniquely human tasks into a standard mold generally just causes them to fail. A performer doesn't succeed merely by regurgitating a script. Teaching is far down the spectrum toward the arts, where standardized protocols generally get in the way of effectiveness.

Systematizing schools is part of a broader modern fallacy about the power of organization, a phenomenon that practically guarantees failure precisely because it severs humans from their instincts. We must "get to the heart of reality through personal experience," Vaclav Havel observes, not with "systems, institutions, mechanisms and statistical averages." It's ironic that a nation founded on the belief in individual freedom should work so hard to program human choices. But that's what we've done, and now we must undo it.

Education is a profoundly personal enterprise. Some people will be good at it. Some will not be. Having good teachers five years in a row, Stanford economist Eric Hanushek found, could eliminate the average achievement gap between poor students and their higher-income peers. It works in reverse as well: Three consecutive years of bad teaching, another study found, will cause students to lag more than fifty percentage points behind peers with good teaching. "Of all the factors we study—class size, ethnicity, location, poverty—" Professor William Sanders found, "they all pale to triviality in the face of teacher effectiveness."

So why not organize a plan to get good teachers? That's what Congress tried to do with the No Child Left Behind Law, which requires states to have in every classroom teachers who are "certified," basically that teachers have pass through various academic hoops, such as having a graduate degree or passed state competency examinations. The idea, in the words of the congressional committee report, was "to ensure all teachers teaching . . . are highly qualified by the end of the 2005–2006 school year."

What a great idea! But it doesn't work. The organizational presumption—that teacher credentials are an indicator of effectiveness—turns out to be inaccurate. In an evaluation of New York City teachers in 2005, Harvard Professor Thomas Kane found no correlation between certification and a teacher's effectiveness. Nor did academic pedigree matter; it made no difference whether the teacher was an Ivy League grad or had gone to a community college. Experience mattered, but far less than you might think. But some teachers, the study found, were dramatically more effective than others. A similar study in Los Angeles found that "whether a teacher is certified or not is largely irrelevant to predicting his or her effectiveness."

What makes a good teacher? Some people just seem to have a knack for it. It's a matter of personality. Management expert Peter Drucker observed that "in teaching we rely on the 'naturals,' the ones who somehow know how to teach." "Anyone who has set foot in a classroom as anything other than a pupil," an editorial in *Teacher Magazine* noted, will know that "it is mostly the teacher's personality that creates and maintains a space in which learning can take place." Drucker also understood that this knack could not be taught: "Teaching is the only major occupation of man for which we have not yet developed tools that make an average person capable of competence and performance."

In *The Moral Life of Schools*, Philip Jackson and colleagues at the University of Chicago studied how teachers succeeded. The diversity of approach was astonishing. One effective teacher, Mrs. Walsh, was charismatic—a "stately, well-dressed, flamboyantly dramatic and enthusiastic teacher," described by the observer as a "high priestess of ninth-grade English." Mr. Turner, also a high school English teacher, came into the classroom disheveled and disorganized and quietly shuffled through a mess of papers before finally asking the class where they had left off. Then there ensued an extraordinary discussion about biblical metaphors in *Moby-Dick*.

Each of us can probably tell similar stories. The good teachers I remember connected with their students by looking them in the eye. That look spoke volumes. Professor Jackson found the same thing. The students "spend a lot of time looking at the teacher. They look to find out how a teacher 'takes' things, to see whether it's safe to laugh at another student's smart-alecky remark or whether their own cleverness has evoked an appreciative response." Professor Jackson observed that "the look on the teacher's face is frequently the key to understanding what's going on. . . . Looks of kindness, impatience, good humor, sternness, incredulity, indignation, pity, discouragement, disapproval, delight, admiration, surprise, disbelief—the list could easily go on—are all part of the teacher's normal repertoire."

A successful personality for teaching requires, as a first condition, that teachers are free to be themselves. "The way a teacher enters the room or the way he or she stands about while waiting for the class to come to order," Professor Jackson noted, conveys a sense of who she is and her authority over the classroom. When Mrs. Walsh, the high priestess of ninth-grade English, was interrupted by a booming voice of the principal over the loudspeaker, she immediately reeled away from the loudspeaker, clasping her heart as if about to faint from shock. The class erupted in laughter.

Just as good teachers can't be produced like widgets on an assembly line, the way they teach can't be programmed. There is merit to pedagogical ideas and other educational techniques, but teaching is mainly about the *delivery* of those ideas. With good teachers, students do not see a teaching machine, extruded from graduate school spouting the same words and techniques, but a live individual, with values, idiosyncrasies, and the spontaneity that comes from freedom. Scripted responses are the antithesis of what's needed to build a culture.

Schools in America are organized on a profound misunderstanding of the human factor in teaching and learning. We're teaching children to help them through life. Life is not mainly about protocols. Nor is life a multiple-choice exam. Life is about values, and social interaction, and discipline, and individuality, and a million other things that bureaucracy can't control. Schools exist to help teach our children these things, not to satisfy a bureaucratic god that everything is done the same way. "How can you convince kids that you are interested in their well-being," Manhattan Institute's Kay Hymowitz observes, "when from day one of the school year you feel bureaucratic pressure to speak with them in a legalistic or quasi-therapeutic gobbledygook rather than a simple moral language they can understand?"

The depersonalized organization of schools rests not on the laurels of its success (obviously), but on an unspoken and powerful premise: that law requires school choices to be standardized. Public schools, after all, are an arm of government. Only with detailed codes can we be sure everyone is treated the same. But schools are not a regulatory agency, requiring legal standards to protect against state authority. Schools are a service, not unlike public transit, that happens to be provided by government. Yes, schooling should be available to everyone. But that doesn't require standardizing every decision in a classroom.

But what about fairness? Our culture is so guilt-ridden and distrustful that we can barely stomach the idea that a principal or teacher might actually have the authority to decide what's fair. But if law were really needed for fundamental fairness—for example, as environmental standards are needed to establish thresholds for industrial processes—then presumably this law should apply to private and parochial schools as well. Disciplining a student is not akin to criminal conviction—the principal is sending the student home, not to jail. Fairness in schools—an essential element of a healthy school culture—requires assertion of values by the people in charge, not application of rules *against* the people in charge.

The Supreme Court has stated numerous times, when requiring due process in schools, that it didn't mean to turn schools into regulatory agencies. But injecting legal analysis into ordinary daily decisions is debilitating. Here is some migraine-inducing language from the Court that is supposed to guide educators on what's required:

> All that [due process] required was an "informal give-and-take" between the student and the administrative body dismissing him that would, at least, give the student "the opportunity to characterize his conduct and put it in what he deems the proper context." . . . The need for flexibility is well illustrated by the significant difference between the failure of

a student to meet academic standards and the violation by a student of valid rules of conduct. This difference calls for far less stringent procedural requirements in the case of an academic dismissal.

Now you begin to see the problem—due process is different for grading than for discipline. Where does a principal go to figure out how much process is due?

Once law enters daily choices, it keeps pouring in, like water through a leak. All day long teachers make choices—about grades, comportment, participation in sports and clubs—that affect students. If teachers and principals don't have the authority to do what they think is right, at least not without a legal proceeding, then they might as well have no authority at all. Supreme Court Justice Lewis Powell, dissenting in one of the early due process cases, warned that this would be the effect: "Few rulings would interfere more extensively in the daily functioning of schools than subjecting routine discipline to the formalities and judicial oversight of due process." Justice Powell's law clerk at the time, Joel Klein, is now suffering through the reality of that prediction as chancellor of New York City schools.

School organization is essential as a platform on which human activity can occur; it provides the classrooms and other infrastructure, tells everyone to show up on time, imposes a common pedagogy so students can progress from year to year, and mandates uniform testing to measure academic progress. But none of those organizational requirements, done properly, requires conscious thought during the day; they all are readily internalized. Once an organizational structure makes teachers focus on compliance rather than on students, the school starts to fail.

Schools are human institutions. Each teacher is different. Each student is different, with different capabilities, interests, and background. The complexity of creating a nurturing learning experience defies description. Teaching draws on every resource of emotion, perception, and experience. The chances of success are uniquely dependent on particular humans. Teachers and principals must be free to use all these resources, all the time.

RESTORE TEACHER RESPONSIBILITY

Deerlake Middle School in Tallahassee, Florida, regularly has the highest test scores in Florida. Unlike TEAM Academy in Newark, it has the advantage of serving a middle-class community with few cultural land mines. But Deerlake still stands out among the thousands of schools that could boast similar advantages: It was one of only thirteen middle schools in the country to earn the No Child Left Behind blue ribbon award in 2005. Its competitive advantage, by all accounts, is the culture created by its principal for many years, Jackie Pons. His operating philosophy is virtually identical to that at TEAM Academy: Let the teachers do what they think makes sense.

"We've got to get away from forcing teachers to conform to this systematic style," Pons noted. "Florida has so many policies and procedures—we've legislated ourselves to the point that teachers have lost room for creativity and freedom." "We've taken so much away from teachers, so much responsibility. . . . Little things like even signing in and signing out. Bigger things like how to run a classroom. . . . Remember, classrooms are most effective when students have strong feelings about their teachers. It's the engagement! We have traditional teachers who are very successful. And we also have younger, innovative teachers trying and succeeding with a whole range of difficult techniques, different styles."

Most of us probably think that power is a zero-sum game. Either it's mine or it's yours. But in successful schools and, indeed, in every successful joint endeavor, that's not how it works. People are empowered not by securing rights over others but by commitment to a common cause. A principal who lets teachers try things on their own will see lots of new ideas, some of which will be successful. Other ideas will be flops. A lesson is learned from those as well. "When you give freedom away," Pons observed, "it comes back to you ten times over. Teachers start taking responsibility for every single student."

Any effective "principle of management," Peter Drucker observed, must "give full scope to individual strength and responsibility." That's what Sara Lightfoot found in *The Good High School*, her study of successful high schools in the 1980s. Bob Mastruzzi, the principal at the time at John F. Kennedy High School in the Bronx, "not only encourages faculty creativity and autonomy, but . . . also allows people the room to make mistakes." He explained: "I want to have as many people as possible join in deciding and acting. They must become responsible for something larger than themselves. . . . I'm willing to tolerate the inefficiency because in the end, people will feel more connected, more committed and pulled into the process."

Freedom to think for themselves is the first thing teachers at good schools talk about. One nineteen-year veteran in a high-poverty school in California emphasized the importance of "being able to pace my presentation of the curriculum and not having to be on such-and-such a page on day 38. Kids don't fit into nice little molds like that." Ryan Hill at TEAM Academy gave an example of how fairness can require different penalties for the same conduct. "We have one boy who will laugh at mistakes by other kids, but he really doesn't know that he is hurting someone. There are other kids who are deliberately being mean. We have to handle those situations differently."

Giving people responsibility energizes the entire enterprise. "We change everything all the time," Heidi Moore at TEAM Academy observed. "Kids' needs change every day. And we have the power, if something really amazing happens, if kids have a really incredible achievement, or if something serious happens—we can decide as a team at lunch to have an all-school assembly, to gather the kids together as a community to talk about it. We have the power to do that. You have to have the power to abandon your schedule."

Strong principals are essential in successful schools because they act as buffers against bureaucracy. "I get things from the district that I'm required to do," Jackie Pons from Deerlake Middle School in Tallahassee observed, "and I just refuse to do them." That's also how Bob Mastruzzi from Kennedy High School in the Bronx worked; as one teacher there put it, "We have a great deal of freedom here . . . [because] Mastruzzi protects his faculty from the arbitrary regulations of the central authority. . . . He serves as a buffer." Another principal similarly concluded: "Trust is a big part of any vision. Teachers . . . know it is okay to make mistakes and the roof won't cave in."

Restoring personal responsibility is the key to fixing America's schools. Teachers and principals must be liberated to think and do what they think is best for their students. It would be hard to find a successful school that's worked in any other way. We must abandon the bureaucracy. In its place we should build a simple framework that requires humans to take responsibility, supporting those that are good at it and holding accountable those who are not. The challenge, as with most human endeavor, is in execution. These should be the governing principles:

1. *Free the teachers (and every other adult).* Every school should be able to manage itself independently, as if it were a charter school. People need the freedom to be themselves and to build their own culture. The benefits will be immediate: energy, resourcefulness, pride, and an accurate sense that success is now up to you. "I'm sure it's true for you and it's certainly true for me," Ryan Hill observed. "I've never met anyone who didn't want to be in charge of their destiny."

Public schools should basically have no different legal constraints from other schools in society. Schools can be given goals and be accountable to officials up the chain of responsibility. But educators on the ground must be free to make the day-to-day choices needed to accomplish those goals. Instead of a rulebook, schools should have a one- or two-page constitution, with broad principles.

But what to do about the huge bureaucracy? Just shove the rulebooks to the side for a while. This can be done with broad waivers passed by the legislatures. As schools begin to function more effectively, the rules become vestigial and can be disposed of in a wholesale way.

2. *Don't tolerate disorder.* Order and respect for authority are essential for a healthy school culture. Nothing gets fixed, almost nothing gets learned, as long as there is disorder. "Five percent of the kids in the classroom, or at most ten percent . . . ruin education for everyone else," noted former Massachusetts Board of Education member Abigail Thernstrom. This can't be allowed to continue. Principals and teachers need the authority to act promptly to remove disruptive students—without stopping to fill out forms or worrying about building the record. "In all the [good] schools I visited," Sara Lightfoot observed, "acts of violence were . . . swiftly punished."

The purpose of prompt action in the face of disorder is essential not because the assertion of authority builds a healthy culture—a show of force is itself a sign of weakness—but because it prevents further deterioration. "It is not punishment that gives discipline its authority," Durkheim wrote, "but it is punishment that prevents discipline from losing this authority." Sara Lightfoot describes how Norris Hogans, the principal at George Washington Carver High School in Atlanta, began to build a healthy culture. "Discipline and authority [were] the key to gaining control of a change process. . . . Schools must provide the discipline, the safety, and the resources that these students are not getting at home. . . . Visible conformity, obedience, and a dignified presence are critical."

Some students, for a variety of reasons beyond their control, will not be able to abide by the essential conditions of order. Urban schools are filled, for example, with eighteen-year-olds in ninth-grade classes. This is a formula for trouble—academic humiliation mixed with physical superiority. They should be in another classroom or program, where they can be with peers and explore possible vocational or other skills. Dedicating resources to the students who don't fit into mainstream classrooms may be the most important priority in American education—it's a good investment not only for the students in trouble but for all of society.

What about the unfair principal? Distrust of authority is like a hot iron on our consciousness. Guarding against unfairness can be achieved, however, without legal process. Independent fairness committees exist in many schools, with authority to decide or overturn disciplinary decisions. These committees could consist of parents, students, and/or teachers. The goal is not perfect justice but a check and balance to protect against arbitrary injustice. As with lawsuits, the focus of fairness should be not just the individual in trouble but what's needed to protect all the students. The first priority must be an environment that supports those students who want to learn and are willing to abide by the rules.

3. *Judge schools by their culture.* The goal for America's schools should be to restore the conditions for a healthy school culture, and all that implies, not their performance on isolated criteria. Pig-headed obsessions with test scores, teacher "certification," and other objective criteria have transformed educators into idiot savants, desperately trying to satisfy the criteria without regard to deleterious effects on students or the school culture. "Beneath this admirable rhetoric," philosopher Onora O'Neill has observed, "the real focus is on performance indicators chosen for ease of measurement and control rather than because they measure quality of performance accurately."

Judging a school requires subjective perceptions. That's true with most important decisions in social interaction, especially (as I shortly discuss) those involving accountability—including whether a teacher is effective or an essay is well written. Evaluating schools is not that hard—educators say they can begin to tell whether a school's any good in a matter of minutes—but it requires the authority to make subjective judgments as well as to look at objective metrics.

Good teachers and principals are a gift to all society. They should be honored, not tied in legal knots and then blamed for failure. The core condition, both for attracting good teachers and for allowing them to succeed, is that they are liberated to be themselves. Their sense of self-worth, like their enthusiasm, will be contagious. "The most important thing [she] communicates," Professor Philip Jackson observed about Mrs. Walsh, the high priestess of ninth-grade English, "is that [she] likes being where she is and doing what she is doing."

Energetic teachers, not bureaucracy, are the building blocks of a healthy school culture. "Too many places look to packaged programs to build visions for learning," as one principal put it. "Well, I say they can't get there that way. . . . Visions have to be homegrown, gradually developed, and based on trust." The California study on teacher retention reaches the same conclusion: "The very process of asking teachers about their schools and soliciting their help in making these schools better places to work is not just a step toward solving a problem—it is an important part of the solution."

American schools need to prepare our children for tough competition in a global society. Teachers are supposed to be role models. Instead our schools radically devalue the human element in making things work. It's as if we were trying to teach our children to fail. Accomplishment is not a multiple-choice test; it's about individual resourcefulness and understanding. American schools have been organized "on the totally erroneous assumption," as management expert Peter Drucker put it, "that there is one right way to learn and it is the same for everyone."

John Stuart Mill observed that a culture "may be progressive for a certain length of time, and then stop: When does it stop? When it ceases to possess individuality." That's what's happened to America's schools. Bureaucracy and legal fear have smothered individuality. This happened because of fears of the dark side of individuality—people can be ineffective, or worse. But the answer to that is also the freedom of individuals—the freedom to hold people accountable. This is the subject of the next chapter.

CHAPTER 6

THE FREEDOM TO JUDGE OTHERS

Liberating teachers from bureaucracy is not all that's needed to make them succeed. Even creating a good culture, as at TEAM Academy, is not enough. A lot depends on the particular person. "We had a teacher here—a really nice guy with great credentials and several years of teaching under his belt—who just couldn't relate to the students," Ryan Hill remembered. "It's hard to put my finger on exactly why. He would blow a little hot and cold, letting one student get away with talking in class and then coming down hard on someone else who did the same thing. . . . But the effect was that the kids started arguing back. It affected the whole school. Kids would come out of his class in a belligerent mood. . . . We worked with him on classroom management the summer after his first year. It usually helps, but he just didn't have the knack. So we had to let him go."

Any healthy organization requires accountability. There's nothing sinister about it. Some people don't work out. It happens all the time, for all kinds of reasons. Most of us pick ourselves up, learn from the experience, and go on to something else.

Someone must make decisions about accountability. Making

these judgments about people, however, is not conducive to objective criteria. Success in a job is certainly not a matter of credentials or logic. How do you prove who has good judgment, or tries hard, or has the knack of running a classroom? People are not like manufactured products, either well made or defective. You can't appraise people in the abstract, Chester Barnard explained in *The Functions of the Executive*. "Men are neither good nor bad, but only good or bad in this or that position." Just think of the variables that apply to each person—aptitude, training, character, energy, personality, caring, to name a few obvious ones. Failure at a job, like success, has infinite permutations. As Professor Philip Jackson notes, teachers can be "kind or cruel, fair or unfair, considerate or inconsiderate, domineering or cooperative, as their fancy or moral temperament suits them."

Group dynamics only compound the complexity of making judgments about people. Whether a person succeeds in a job is often a question of fit. People who succeed in a big organization, Peter Drucker observed, often fail in a small one. A brilliant high school teacher may be terrible with first graders. How a person relates to the other employees is critical. "The question of personal compatibility or incompatibility," Chester Barnard observed, "is much more far reaching in limiting cooperative efforts than is recognized."

We tend to think of accountability from the standpoint of the affected person, but accountability is profoundly a matter of the group. There's nothing more important in an enterprise than how people feel about each other. "A social organism of any sort . . . is what it is," William James noted, "because each member proceeds to his own duty with a trust that the other members will simultaneously do theirs." Camaraderie among employees is the most productive resource any enterprise can have. People row harder if they feel that they're rowing together. When it clicks, there's nothing more powerful than the fellow feeling of people working together for a common goal. In the California study on teacher retention, mutual affinity was second only to "decision-making authority" as the most important factor mentioned by teachers who liked their jobs. "When people identify with the group," organizational psychologists tell us, "they feel a moral duty to cooperate." Soldiers can endure the horrors of war because their buddies are enduring it with them. They face death because they face it together.

But the positive leverage becomes negative when an organization tolerates employees who aren't perceived to be pulling their weight. Ineffective workers not only are deficient in their contribution but also have a corrosive effect on everyone else. A study at the University of Washington found that there is a "precipitous decline in teammate contributions . . . when a single individual free rides." "One bad apple," the study concluded, "can spoil the barrel." The fact that the ineffective person remains is a constant reminder of the lack of mutual obligation. Over time one person can drag down a culture.

Welcome to public employment in America. There is no accountability in America's government service or public schools. This is not a secret. Due process, civil service protections, and union contracts put public employees in a "virtually impregnable position." "Basically whether you perform well or you perform poorly, you are treated the same," New York City Schools Chancellor Joel Klein observes. We might as well have sprayed a depressant into the air of public offices.

Morale plummets when employees see others not doing their jobs. Every teacher, every public servant can tell you horror stories. Betsy Rogers, a former National Teacher of the Year from Alabama, considers almost nothing more discouraging than teachers who don't try. "On a daily basis, I see teachers who start classes late, chatting on their cell phones while they eat breakfast in front of their students. . . . There are even a few classes where I have yet to see any instruction taking place. . . . The sense of pride I felt for the teaching profession [when I received the award] was overwhelming. . . . Today, at the age [of] 54, I finally had to look myself in the mirror and say out loud—There are educators who do not care."

Lack of accountability brings with it an evil twin—growth in bureaucracy. When people can't be judged for *whether* they did the job, pretty soon rules will instruct them on exactly *how* to do the job. Bureaucracy accelerates to warp speed (as it were) as rules strive to keep pace with the unintended consequences. The forms teachers spend hours filling out are just a bureaucratic scolding device, like forcing them to write on the blackboard: "I followed the script. I filled out the evaluations." We are now at the point of total bureaucracy—trying to create "'teacher proof' curriculum . . . consist[ing] of step-by-step lesson plans prescribed in such detail that ostensibly anyone could teach them, no matter how skilled or unskilled."

A common characteristic of public agency culture—particularly in state and municipal bureaucracies—is one of gray powerlessness. People shuffle here and there, going through the motions. There is no pressure to cooperate, to solve problems, to work hard, or to do anything. One of my daughters worked for a summer in the Massachusetts State House, where her job—this was in 2002— was to do an inventory of ancient phones stored in the basement. Who is making the decision to keep telephones that have been collecting dust for decades? My daughter learned one lesson: Don't work in government.

Life within these agencies can be awful. Just cling on to a few rules and entitlements, and drift along for thirty years. Then you'll get a pension. Thirty years in that culture must seem like thirty lifetimes. One public manager told me about a retirement party where, trying to make conversation, he said, "You must have seen some interesting times here." The worker responded, "Not really." The manager tried again and got the same response. "Not really." In "Bartleby the Scrivener," a short story written by Herman Melville about the horror of functionary jobs, the title character responds to each request with a similar passive refusal: "I would prefer not to." The comatose culture of some government departments, where decades of dust settle onto ancient files, is not something normal people want to contemplate. We would prefer not to.

No one even thinks of mounting an assault on this huge legal bulwark that surrounds public employees. It's been this way for so long, largely unquestioned, that we accept this as a fact of nature. It must be guarding something very valuable. Terrible woes, maybe even a return of the spoils system, will befall us unless public employees are insulated from accountability based on—perish the thought—how well they do. Any accountability reform, in the words of a union official, would create "a system open to cronyism and subjectivity." Just think of the abuses if people in public service were accountable to other public servants or, even more shocking, to elected officials.

But maybe that accountability is just what American schools and government need. Today politicians and their appointees blame inept government for our woes. Might it not be better if political leaders actually had the authority to do something about it? Democracy is a chain of authority that ultimately rests upon the vote of the people. Break any links in the chain, and democracy starts to sag. It doesn't matter much whom we elect if they don't have ultimate authority over the competence of officials actually delivering the services. "Public policy is not best understood as made in legislatures or top-floor suites," Michael Lipsky writes in *Street-Level Bureaucracy*, but "in the crowded offices and daily encounters of street-level workers." Nine out of ten decisions needed to get anything done, management expert Chester Barnard observed, are made by the person on the ground. Democracy can't do its job unless those people on the ground are both free to take responsibility and accountable for fulfilling their responsibility.

Accountability is the flip side of freedom. You will be free to act on your best judgment only if others are free to judge you. Otherwise, before you have time to spell b-u-r-e-a-u-c-r-a-c-y, rules will be instituted telling you how to do your job. Freedom doesn't work unless there's freedom all around.

DUE PROCESS ON THE LOOSE AGAIN

Public employees must be protected against unfair management decisions, the argument goes. It's David against Goliath, the small individual against the giant institution. Overprotection is a small price to pay, union leaders say, to avoid unfairness. "We need due process," a teachers' union official argued, "as long as there are people who might fire you because they didn't like what you wore that day." But Goliath isn't the main adversary here. A poor teacher injures all the other Davids in that school, including students and other teachers. Students who are taught by ineffective teachers, as we have seen, will learn only a fraction of what other students do.

It's just a matter of proof, union leaders say: "Tenure simply requires due process, meaning a chance to hear and respond to charges. . . . This concept is one of the foundations of American democracy." Here we go again: Are you against teachers' rights? In the heyday of the rights revolution, in the 1960s and 1970s, the Supreme Court expanded the reach of the due process clause to personnel decisions for public employees. The basic idea is that competence can be proved in a legal hearing. "It is not burdensome to give reasons," as Justice Thurgood Marshall put it, "when reasons exist."

It's easy enough to give reasons. Unfortunately, it's also easy to disagree with them. Whatever you call these protections, they are not "just a matter of due process" or "just" anything. Years of legal argument—*years*—are required to get rid of a bad teacher. In 2004 Common Good did an analysis of how many steps it took to dismiss a teacher in New York. The chart, filled with tiny bubbles representing each legal consideration, was five feet long. A similar study in Denver, describing an actual termination proceeding, produced a chart almost as long. The school board succeeded in firing a teacher for refusing to teach the required courses—after a legal process lasting twenty-seven months.

These legal safeguards against accountability are cloaked in rhetoric that bears almost no relation to reality. Fairness to the particular teacher is the stated goal. But fairness, as we've seen, also involves considering the fairness to students and fairness to the other teachers. And what is the standard of performance for fairness in the workplace? The judge or hearing officer needs some benchmark principle against which to evaluate the facts. Is it competence? Mediocrity? The bare minimum?

For teachers and public employees, the standard is lower than the bare minimum. Any sliver of rationalization is often good enough to keep a job. In East St. Louis, an assistant principal who impregnated a fourteen-year-old student was ordered reinstated on the basis that the evidence was not conclusive; years later, when DNA tests established his paternity to a 99 percent certainty, he was suspended again but allowed to apply for recertification. A teacher in New Jersey acted inappropriately on a regular basis, for example, referring to a student as "your typical nigger" and "created such a negative learning environment" that some students couldn't sleep at night. The correct procedure, the state commissioner of education found, was to order her to go to anger management classes.

Government agencies have the same problem. Cincinnati basically lost control of its police force because it couldn't fire anyone. The arbitrators who were charged with making the decision always found a reason for giving someone another chance. One police dispatcher—terminated for forgetting to dispatch police, placing emergencies on hold, falling asleep, and using crime lines for personal calls—was ordered reinstated because of extenuating circumstances—a toothache and a difficult pregnancy. A policeman fired for being drunk on the job and trying to pull a revolver on someone in a bar was ordered reinstated on the basis that alcoholism is a disease.

Life is about aspiration. Law is generally about the minimum. That's why due process, so noble-sounding, is poisonous in the workplace. Instead of judging against a standard of excellence, due process looks to the lowest acceptable standard: Is this person so bad that he should lose his job? In a society that strives to get As, due process protects people who get Ds. That's how due process is supposed to work—it's designed to *prevent* decisions (specifically, to prevent the state from taking away our property or throwing us in jail). That's certainly how employment cases are argued— a person's performance is judged against the worst employee the litigant can find. "Mediocrity is not a sin," former Denver Superintendent of Schools Jerry Wartgow observes; "it's a guarantee of life employment."

The debate over teacher tenure has all the dynamics of World War I: both sides dug in, going nowhere, hurling nasty attacks at each other. It's been going on so long that no one in memory has actually stepped back and calmly discussed what the fight's about. Look at how little they're fighting over. "No one wants teachers who are not pulling their weight," union leader Randi Weingarten acknowledges. Unless principals and other supervisors are idiots or are really insecure (some are, I know), they don't have an incentive to get rid of good people. And if a teacher is in fact good, she won't have much of a problem getting a new job.

So what is this holy war really about? It's about ideology, specifically that teachers have a right to a legal trial before losing their jobs. The ideology springs from the toxic combination of union protectionism and the 1960s' expansion of due process. Due process was supposed to add a kind of gold plating to employee protections. It worked better than anyone could have imagined—it sealed off the oxygen of honest interaction. Due process supposedly protects the employees. Would you like to trade places with a public school teacher?

Both sides are dug in so deep that they can't see how this went wrong. There's an assumption that worker protection is all or nothing—it's either no protection or a full legal arsenal against accountability. But that isn't the only choice. Indeed, the original goal of civil service, and of labor protections, and even of civil rights laws, was not to protect against individual accountability decisions. The purpose was to protect against group-wide abuses—for example, abusive working conditions. The distinction is critical. Protecting against group-wide abuses creates a safe and level playing field without paralyzing personal accountability.

PROTECTING GROUPS, NOT INDIVIDUALS

One of the triumphs of law in the twentieth century was to elevate protections for workers and consumers over the nineteenth-century legal doctrines of laissez-faire and caveat emptor. The Industrial Revolution created forces far too powerful for people to defend against without legal protection. Generations of legal reformers devoted their lives to protecting people against the abuses of huge corporate and governmental organizations.

These were, and are, necessary protections. Restoring personal accountability does not mean that employers can return to the bad old days of worker abuse or racism. Lost in the haze of history, however, is the fact that none of these historic reforms originated as protections of individuals. These reforms all were aimed at protecting against conduct that affected an entire category of people, not at protecting the job of a particular person. The civil rights movement was aimed at tearing down the walls of segregation, for example, not at allowing a legal case any time a person lost his job. But each historic reform ended up getting captured by the protected group and transformed into a shield against personal accountability.

The lines can blur, of course, like most legal lines. But the focus is entirely different. Today the idea of rights focuses on sympathy for the individual. "This is someone's job, someone's career. It's how he supports his family. Just give him one more chance." That legal logic soon slides down to a place where inept teachers and sleeping police dispatchers have a legal entitlement to inflict their failures on society. Protecting groups is entirely different. The focus is on systemic abuses, not disagreements over the performance of one person. The question is not fairness to the particular person—which opens the door to litigation over virtually any adverse workplace decision—but whether the decision reflects a bias or abusive practice against the group.

Protecting against unfair workplace practices started in the 1880s with the creation of civil service, safeguarding the public against the corruption of the spoils system, in which government jobs essentially had been sold to the party faithful. With patronage there was no requirement that the person actually do the job well (or, in some jobs, even show up at all). Creating a civil service meant that government employees would be hired on the basis of merit by a neutral commission. That's why it was called the merit system.

Civil servants were not supposed to be immune from accountability. The goal was to neutralize hiring, not interfere with accountability decisions. Dismissal remained a matter of discretion. With patronage eliminated, there was no ulterior motive to fire good workers. "If the front door is well-guarded," reformers believed, "the back door will take care of itself." The first head of the Civil Service Commission, George William Curtis, was explicit on the need for personal accountability: "It is better to take the risk of occasional injustice . . . than to seal up incompetency, negligence, insubordination, insolence and every other mischief in the service by requiring a virtual trial at law before an unfit and incapable clerk can be removed."

But the new class of civil servants amassed their own political power; after all, elected leaders couldn't do anything without them. Within two decades civil servants had succeeded in securing layers of job security. Theodore Roosevelt, an original civil service reformer, was furious to discover that as president he had no authority to get rid of people not doing the job. Zell Miller confronted the same problem when he became governor of Georgia: "Too often in government, we pass laws to fix particular problems of the moment, and then we allow half a century to roll by without ever following up to see what the long-term consequences have been. Folks, the truth of the matter is that . . . despite its name, our present Merit System is not about merit. It offers no reward to good workers. It only provides cover for bad workers."

The labor movement similarly arose to protect the group—in that case, from unsafe and inhumane working conditions and wages. Going to work every day was a little like going off to war, with death and disfigurement commonplace. In the 1870s, 12 percent of anthracite coal miners in Pennsylvania were killed or permanently disabled each year; in the 1890s, one in a hundred railroad brakemen died each year. The rise of the labor movement changed work conditions so that workers were treated like people, not like machine parts that could be worn out and discarded. As labor unions amassed power, however, they flexed their muscles to get as much as they could—and started protecting individuals from accountability. Workers kept jobs even when there were no jobs for them. Union contracts required firemen on diesel locomotives when there was no coal to shovel. But as competitive pressures mounted in the mid-twentieth century, union leaders realized that union jobs depended on the employers' efficiency. Today personal accountability is not generally a problem in unionized industrial companies; the union shop steward and co-workers don't want slackards or misfits any more than the company does.

The greatest of these reform efforts was the civil rights movement. The civil rights movement set out to open up all public accommodations and to allow minorities to compete for jobs. But it had almost nothing to do with judgments about particular individuals. Hubert Humphrey and other sponsors of the Civil Rights Act of 1964 took pains to emphasize that the act was intended to remove artificial barriers based on race or gender, not to give employees affirmative rights to require employers to hire them.

With civil rights, as with all these reforms, the momentum kept reformers pushing for ever more protection. The pace of integration was slower than had been hoped for, and the reformers decided to take the battle down to each workplace decision. Each individual would be provided a legal sword to fight for his right to the job he thought he deserved. In 1991 Congress amended civil rights laws to "encourage citizens to act as private attorneys general," including authorizing jury trials and payment of attorneys' fees. For lawyers, as one put it, this was "manna from heaven." Laws prohibiting discrimination against the disabled and the elderly were passed at roughly the same time. The effect was as intended—a threefold increase in employment discrimination claims by 1997.

The goal of discrimination law had now changed. Discrimination law was no longer focused on patterns of discrimination, but had become a general law of workplace fairness—over 70 percent of workers are in some "protected category." In 2003 the blind director of Pennsylvania's agency for the blind was terminated and replaced by another woman with impaired eyesight. But that didn't keep the dismissed director from suing and winning a $3.4 million verdict that she had been discriminated against on the basis of her disability. Who is law supposed to be protecting, the protected person losing the job or the protected person getting the job? It doesn't really matter, because discrimination law is available to be used as a lever for personal vindication, not protecting the interests of the particular group.

Invoking law to protect against individual accountability is entirely different from using law to protect against group-wide practices. In the glory days of the civil rights movement, lawsuits knocked down barriers by proving patterns and practices of discrimination—such as at the steelworkers' union, where the court found that "job assignment practices were reprehensible," or at the supermarket chain that never promoted any female cashiers. These cases turned on demonstrable factual patterns.

Lawsuits over individual accountability, by contrast, rarely turn on discrete legal or factual issues—how do you prove or disprove who is effective? Judges nonetheless require employers to come up with objective proof for judgments that are generally a matter of subjective perception. "A remarkably wide range of qualities are considered too subjective to stand up in court," Walter Olson notes in *The Excuse Factory*, including such characteristics as "temperament, habits, demeanor, bearing, manner, maturity, drive, leadership ability, personal appearance, stability, cooperativeness, dependability, adaptability, industry, work habits, attitude . . . and interest in job."

The flaws of bringing law down to personal judgments quickly become apparent when the lawsuit begins. A lawsuit over individual accountability turns into a trial over the person's worth, like a trial over life itself. Having to "prove" why a person isn't working out in a job—whether for incompetence, a bad attitude, or a thousand other traits—transforms accountability into a kind of divorce proceeding, boiling over with emotion. "You say I acted inappropriately? Well, how bad was it? Don't other people act inappropriately sometimes? I think it has to be discrimination. Why didn't I get those plum assignments?"

Putting individual accountability into a legal cauldron is a recipe for bitterness, obsession, and fear. The supervisor, co-workers, and lawyers spend months trying to construct a case with objective proof of incompetence and bad judgment. All this is recorded in affidavits and deposition transcripts. The personal disappointment of the job not working out, which would be quickly forgotten if the individual just got a new job, becomes a crusade on both sides. The claim ends up consuming the life of the person supposedly protected. After all, it's a trial over your inherent quality as a person. Moving on to a new job would be so much less painful (and less expensive) than throwing your character onto the pyre of legal justification.

The overhang of law in workplace decisions has changed the culture. In some ways, the changes have been for the better—employers are more measured in their approach to accountability—but these benefits can probably be accomplished without the backdrop of a holy war. The legal fear in the workplace, however, has unleashed waves of unintended costs. The chilling of honest interaction is palpable, harming most those who are supposedly protected. Distrust replaces candor, starting a downward spiral of misunderstanding. Black workers often talk about an invisible barrier separating them from others in the workplace, as if they had a contagious disease. Spontaneity is replaced by heavy pauses and formalism. Managers and co-workers are afraid not just of lawsuits, but of being labeled bigots. "When avoiding offense becomes our primary concern," Professor Mark Notturno notes, "it quickly becomes impossible to say anything freely at all." Jonathan Rauch sums up the problem this way:

> Daily life in a dense and diverse society is full of moral disputes and interpersonal collisions. Civilized life must be reasonably free of the fear that these everyday disputes and collisions may, at any moment and for no clear reason, suddenly explode into intolerable ordeals.

The effects of this legal self-consciousness ripple into important decisions. Employers say they often won't take a chance on a minority candidate out of fear that they can't dismiss him without risking a discrimination claim. This is a variation of the paradox identified by former Czech president Vaclav Havel as "enforced proximity" that serves mainly to drive people apart.

The myth that law can sort out the truth in human relations lives on. At a hearing before the House Judiciary Committee in 2005, I was asked by Congresswoman Maxine Waters whether I believed anyone would go to the trouble of bringing a discrimination claim if it weren't true. I bit my tongue, and replied only that most federal judges seemed to be of that view. The numbers in fact are overwhelming. There is a dramatic mismatch between the flood of employment claims (10 percent of the federal civil docket) and the probability of success (about 15 percent).

Law can protect against group abuses, but it can't resolve individual disagreements in the workplace without removing the conditions and benefits of free interaction. Some people do things one way; others another way. Some people will get along in the department; others won't. People need to be able to make these choices.

THE VIRTUES OF ACCOUNTABILITY

In 1996, Georgia Governor Zell Miller performed a minor miracle of public administration—he sponsored a law that eliminated civil service protections for new state employees. The benefits were seen immediately. "It was like somebody turned on the lights," observed Paul Burkhalter, the deputy commissioner of the state's Department of Natural Resources. Burkhalter said that his environmental agency always had good people, but there was always the overhang of "knowing that you didn't have to extend yourself." No more. "On snowy days in the north Georgia mountains, civil servants often called in saying they couldn't make it to work," Joe Tanner, a top aide to Governor Miller, recalled. "The new employees somehow made it to work."

Another benefit was to open up opportunities. The fact that jobs were no longer cast in stone meant that supervisors could try people out in higher responsibilities. Burkhalter, a state employee for thirty years and an African-American, moved from a back-office position to being second in charge of the environmental agency. "I wouldn't be here today but for that change in law." Attitudes changed from compliance to accomplishment: "People started thinking about what they could do, not what was required." Accountability stopped being a problem. Even employees still in the classified civil service (now only 15 percent at the environmental agency) will accept discipline and demotions without legal fuss. "I don't even remember the last time we had a problem when someone didn't do their job," Burkhalter noted.

Discussing the virtues of accountability is a little like talking

about the joy of taking exams. It's not exactly what we look forward
to in life. Accountability is scary—someone else judging how we're
doing. "Responsibility does not always bring joy in its wake," Mark
Bovens observes in *The Quest for Responsibility*. "It goes together
. . . with stress, anxiety, and a certain amount of self-sacrifice." But
accountability is an essential part of a healthy life and a healthy
society. We all know this. In this age of legal insecurity, however,
we are no longer free to act on the obvious—as with our obsessions with safety and with rights. We want a perfect world, without
failures or disagreements.

In striving for this utopia we don't notice all the vital benefits
that we lose. The freedom of people to make accountability judgments is vital to just about everything important and joyful in work
life. Here's a partial list:

1. Personal fulfillment. The pride of a job well done is dramatically enhanced by recognition by others. Humans, at least most
of us, long for the approval of others. To be rewarding, this recognition must be earned by genuine accomplishment. A culture
without accountability is dispiriting. "It's very frustrating to high
performers not to be held accountable," said Susan Schaeffler,
a former public school teacher who now runs the KIPP schools
in Washington, D.C. "Good teachers want to be sure that people
appreciate the value they bring to the building."

2. Avoiding self-delusion. To see ourselves as we really are, we
need the mirror of other people's views. Scientists tell us that most
people are incapable of accurately judging themselves, because
humans are hard-wired by nature to be self-centered. Our founders believed this as well—that "a human being was an atom of self-
interest." By protecting against the judgment of others, modern
personnel law fosters these worst tendencies in humans, starting
a downward spiral. "The more a man indulges in the propen-
sity to blame others or circumstances for his failures," Friedrich

Hayek observed, "the more disgruntled and ineffective he tends to become."

One federal judge told me about presiding over a discrimination trial in which the facts of the worker's incompetence were overwhelming. As the trial progressed, it was clear to everyone in the courtroom that the worker had no claim. When the verdict came in dismissing his claim, however, the employee still couldn't see it. He sat in the courtroom in disbelief, crying in frustration at the injustice that had been done to him. Inside a legal cocoon, people let their imaginations replace reality.

3. Personal growth through failure. "We learn wisdom from failure much more than from success," Victorian reformer Samuel Smiles explained. "We often discover what will do, by finding out what will not do. . . . Probably he who never made a mistake never made a discovery."

Failure doesn't get a lot of attention in our culture. Management gurus churn out books, seemingly by the thousands, on how to succeed (Winning!). I don't recall any on how to deal with failure (Failing!). But failure is not some unusual circumstance, needing a dirge and funeral procession. Failure is the norm, as management expert Chester Barnard observed. Success both for an individual and for an enterprise generally comes after countless adaptations to repeated failures.

It's hard to think of a hero of our time who did not overcome significant failure. Winston Churchill was famous for his early failures: as first lord of the admiralty, planning the disastrous assault on the Dardanelles in World War I; as chancellor of the exchequer, returning to the gold standard in 1924, precipitating a depression. But Churchill was right about Germany's rearmament and, after a decade out to pasture, came back to lead Britain in its most perilous hours. To Churchill, success consisted of "moving from failure to failure without loss of enthusiasm."

4. A dynamic economy. Accountability is a key element of a dynamic economy. Americans change jobs, on average, ten times between the ages of twenty and forty. Job movement is the occupational version of trial and error, increasing the odds that people will find a find a place that fits their aptitude and interests. A new personal challenge generally results in higher energy and new skills.

Success in a crowded society is not doing whatever you want but, usually, doing whatever you can persuade other people to let you do. Co-workers constantly judge the performance of people who work with them—about who's doing the job, and who is not, about who works well with others and whose elbows are too sharp. On the open field of freedom, people push and pull each other constantly. That's the dynamic of a free society. "In democracies men are never stationary," Tocqueville observed. "A thousand forces waft them to and fro."

5. Responsibility. I'd like a nickel for each time someone says that Americans need to take more personal responsibility. I'm obviously a fan of responsibility. But how do you get people to act more responsibly? In a free country there's no law against being pushy or selfish or having bad morals. People in a free society are allowed to be sloppy in their work, temperamental, quick to blame others, and less than responsible. Within broad boundaries, on the field of freedom, law will not intervene to help us deal with these issues. We're on our own. The culture we live in and bequeath to our children depends on how we apply our values in daily interaction. If these irresponsible people are allowed to throw up a legal shield against being held accountable, then our values are just hot air, without practical significance.

Accountability, not law, is the key to responsibility. Bureaucracy certainly doesn't get us responsibility. The legalistic mind-set encourages compliance with rules instead of doing what's right.

Legislating individual rights, as with special education, is even worse. Rights promote selfishness, not responsibility. There's only one clear path to responsibility in social dealings: Let people be free to make judgments about each other. Most people want to do the right thing. It's a lot easier if you know that everyone is subject to the same oversight.

6. Ethics. Society's cloak of responsible values, ethics, similarly frays from disuse. The ethics of relativism are basically that it's not fair to assert ethical values. The theory of neutral values is self-defeating, as philosopher Alisdair McIntyre and others have observed, because it allows social values to be dominated by people who don't share the goal of neutrality. Every social enterprise suffers if people aren't free to be "judgmental" on the basis of their sense of responsible ethics. I was debating some legal scholars a few years ago in Richmond, and the subject of lawyer advertising came up. The Supreme Court held (unwisely, in my view) that lawyers have a First Amendment right to advertise, and the scholars argued that since the speech was lawful, nothing could be done about it. But why didn't respectable bar associations, I suggested, exclude ambulance chasers from membership? "What are you going to do," retorted one professor, "shun them?" Actually yes, I replied. Any "profession" worthy of that appellation should enforce what it views as good professional values, irrespective of legality. Isn't that the role of ethics?

Accountability is mainly a concept of risk, not security, at least from the standpoint of the individual. But that individual risk is precisely what makes accountability indispensable to the healthy culture of the group. Moreover, the vicissitudes inherent in accountability are what makes it indispensable to our personal development.

I suspect each of you reading this has a story of some unpleasant collision with accountability that helped form your character.

As a young lawyer I worked for a large New York law firm, and looked forward to a long career there. One weekend, near the time in my career when partnership decisions were made, I received a desperate plea from the New York City landmarks commissioner to try to stop demolition of the Biltmore Hotel, which was scheduled to become a landmark the next week. When I dragged into the office on Monday, after a weekend of securing injunctions, I was greeted with a stack of messages from partners. Who gave me permission to do this? There was no conflict with firm clients (several senior partners had helped me find the judge), but some partners believed this highlighted a disturbing trend. Was I really dedicated to the firm? There ensued months of painful discussion, which ended with my losing my job.

This was not what I had in mind. I had invested eight years of all-nighters in my career there. I had a big mortgage and a second baby on the way. How would I support my family? But losing my job was, without question, the best professional thing that ever happened to me. I had to figure out for myself what I wanted, not just float along in a career defined by others. I learned not to be afraid of failure. You can pick yourself up. Why not take risks? I thought it was unfair at the time, but my old firm was probably correct that I didn't quite fit in. My leaving may have been good for them. It certainly was for me.

Our pioneer forefathers would be amused by the delicate stature we accord job status. America's vitality comes from people fending for themselves. Jobs are about being persuasive or likable, selling whatever needs to be sold, working hard and then working harder, failing and then picking yourself up. Jobs are not precious objects, like fine crystal never to be tossed about. Americans, as noted, change jobs all the time. In Europe, by contrast, jobs have a permanent stature. In past centuries European feudal cultures had vassals, tradesmen in guilds, and the nobility, all stuck in their places for life. Now Europe has laws that make it impossible to fire anyone. People in Europe cling to their jobs as if they were on a respirator. Imagine living in France—in the luggage factory for life. It's not a good system. That's one of the reasons their economy grows at barely more than half the rate of ours.

Too much security makes people fat and unhappy. Too little security is not good either; people shouldn't fear the loss of health care for their families if their jobs don't work out. But either way, there must always be the overhang of accountability. "From child-hood onward," Professor Mark Bovens observes, "our conduct is influenced by the fact that we can be called to account for our actions."

RESTORING THE FREEDOM TO JUDGE PEOPLE

During his sixteen-year nursing career, Charles Cullen worked as a nurse in Pennsylvania and New Jersey, moving from one hospital to the next. He was not a good nurse. He acted strangely and was found in rooms of patients with medications that weren't appro-priate. In most hospitals he never lasted more than a few months before he was let go. But he kept getting new jobs. In 2003 it was discovered that Cullen had probably murdered more than forty patients.

Cullen was able to move from one hospital to another—to ten medical facilities in all—because fear of a lawsuit prevented those hospitals from giving him a bad reference. Co-workers observed his strange behavior, but they didn't know he was murdering peo-ple and couldn't prove that he was doing something illegal. So the hospitals eventually let him go and, when the next hospital in line asked for a reference, merely gave the stock response of all employers nowadays: "We confirm that he worked here from this to that date."

The Pennsylvania state agency overseeing nurses had been warned about Cullen's penchant for diverting medications but, even after the murders had come to light, would not comment on his reputation. "Legally, we can't speak about any information we receive that doesn't result in disciplinary action," a spokesman said.

"What I'm coming to understand," said Dr. William Cors, the chief medical officer of Somerset Medical Center in Somerville, New Jersey, where Cullen last worked, "is that, short of an actual conviction or revocation of license, none of this information gets shared. If anything good comes from this, it would be to reform the system where we're prevented from telling one another what we know out of fear, quite frankly, of being sued."

Virtually every tragedy of this sort—for example, the shootings at Columbine High and Virginia Tech—was committed by people who were known to be unbalanced. Yet no one felt free to do what was obvious and get them out of the institution. Never underestimate the power of prevailing ideology—even sinister people are not allowed to be judged. Our motives are pure: to avoid judging people on the basis of the color of their skin or other superficial criteria. Having to *prove* your judgment, however, is paralyzing: "Just demonstrate that you are being fair. Maybe Cullen is just a little strange. What's wrong with that? Aren't people allowed to be different in a free society?" Put yourselves in the shoes of the hospital director in New Jersey. How exactly would you prove that Nurse Cullen makes your skin crawl?

Legal proceedings can't possibly capture concepts like character or caring. That's why proving the fairness of accountability is a hopeless exercise. Even scientists know little about how we judge people. Human judgment, already a mystery, is even more mysterious when one judges others—a black box making judgments about another black box. But we know the judgments aren't random. Studies show that diverse groups of people, asked to watch a panel of different people talking, tend to trust and distrust the same ones. The correlation remained high when another test group judged the same people with the sound turned off. Jacob Marschak, a prominent economist, hired people in part by watching their eyes: "intelligence shines through the eyes."

"Laying aside all exceptions to the rule, there is typically a lot of truth in the judgments we make of others," Professor Philip Jackson observes in his study of teachers. "This is so even when we cannot quite put our finger on the source of our opinion. That truth, we would suggest, emerges expressively. It is given off by what a person says or does, the way a smile gives an aura of friendliness or tears a spirit of sadness." People "imagine they communicate their virtue or vice only by overt action and do not see that virtue and vice emit a breath every moment," Emerson observed: "We pass for what we are."

As a creature of our rationalist culture you may think it absurd that people should judge others by watching them or by vague feelings about character. But until the last forty years that's been a core precept of civilization. Most great leaders, including George Washington and Abraham Lincoln, were said to have been a "good judge of character." There's a huge library of human wisdom through the ages—by Aristotle, Aquinas, Confucius, Shakespeare, Hume, Martin Luther King, almost everyone we respect—about virtue, character, and other personal traits. All this wisdom is basically useless if people aren't free to make judgments about people.

There's no getting around the judgment of others. Accountability, by definition, is a third-party concept. People get rewarded, Hayek stated, "according to what others think." This idea is repugnant to our modern sensibility. Why should one person be able to judge another? But co-workers are our validation as well as our reality check. The best measure of accountability is impressing others on the job. If you can't please the people around you, then you probably should be somewhere else.

Restoring the conditions for accountability requires a basic shift in law, removing legal walls and weapons that individuals use to insulate themselves and returning to broader principles of group protection. In the public sector what's needed is a kind of mutual disarmament—where the government removes the iron net of bureaucracy and the teachers and other public employees remove their legal armor. Public employees will be liberated to exercise their judgment only when supervisors are liberated to hold them accountable.

NEW DEAL FOR TEACHERS AND PUBLIC EMPLOYEES

Civil service and teacher protections should be largely scrapped and replaced by a new deal. The basic components might be:

1. Protecting against unfairness. Instead of legal hearings and litigation, give a designated person or committee the authority to review and overturn termination decisions—call it the review committee. This would not be a legal proceeding but an informal process of talking with others in the department to make sure there was a reasonable basis for the termination. For schools, the committee might include a parent, a teacher (including a union representative where applicable), and someone from management.

2. Retraining and reassignment opportunities. Large public agencies could provide a program of central evaluation and retraining so that terminated employees have the option of trying to fit in elsewhere. Ultimately, however, the management has to have the authority to weed out those who don't appear to be effective.

3. Safety nets. Today public employees cling to their jobs in part because they don't want to lose health care for their families or give up years of credit toward their pensions. These legitimate concerns should be satisfied. Remove the handcuffs by letting fringe benefits be transferable. Public employees should be vested in their accrued pensions after a threshold period. There could also be a

severance payment based on years of service—providing a disincentive to arbitrary dismissals and a reassurance to employees that they are not at risk of being left high and dry.

4. Neutral hiring and programmed turnover. Going back to the original premise of civil service, career public jobs should be filled through a process based on merit, not connections. But there should also be an expectation that some people will be let go. We will have a hard time encouraging the best people to join and to stay until there is freedom to ask the worst people to leave.

These simple reforms require a legal revolution. Civil service and other laws must be largely repealed and rewritten, the unions must change their requirements, and the Supreme Court must conclude that these kinds of protection satisfy due process. But it's worth the effort. Restoring accountability to public service holds the key to restoring health to our weakened public institutions, including democracy itself.

FAIRNESS IN THE PRIVATE WORKPLACE

A simpler revolution is required to restore balance in the private sector, with the basic shift being a presumption against litigation and a new informal grievance model. Instead of inciting people to sue, law should discourage individual claims. Job references, positive or negative, should not be the basis of a legal claim absent concrete allegations of actual malice (with penalties to the employee for bringing claims that do not meet this standard). Informal review mechanisms, such as mediation, should replace the discrimination and other employment litigation that now engulfs federal courts.

1. Discrimination laws should return to their original purpose, the protection against systematic patterns of discrimination. They can retain their basic prohibitions (although the proliferation of

protected categories, now covering most of the workforce, tends to undermine the protection of racial minorities). Private enforcement should be limited, however, to credible allegations of a pattern or practice of discrimination—lawsuits would be dismissed unless the claimant presented evidence that the employer discriminated against minorities generally, not just against the plaintiff. To safeguard against the occasional individual abuses, a public official should be authorized to bring claims on behalf of individuals. Judges should be given the authority to decide as a matter of law whether allegations meet this threshold. But individuals should not be allowed to bring claims only on behalf of themselves—the overwhelming self-interest and cost of a chilled workplace far outweigh the benefits. The point is not that discrimination has been cured—we all probably harbor subconscious prejudices—but that the unreliability of individual claims freezes the open interaction needed to accomplish real integration.

2. Harassment. These presumptions against individual claims don't work in one situation, sexual harassment. Sexual harassment involves extortion of an individual, not feelings of resentment toward a group. Even here the allegations must rise to a level of quid pro quo, not just offensive comments. Bad taste or humor might be a basis for firing someone but shouldn't be a legal claim. Law can't be pressed down this far without chilling the spontaneity needed for a healthy culture. Sometimes people will put their feet in their mouths. Most people will apologize and get on with life. People can distinguish between missteps by people of good character and mean behavior. "Even a dog," Oliver Wendell Holmes observed, "distinguishes between being stumbled over and being kicked."

3. Employer obligations. Employers too should feel the tension of accountability. As a condition for these limits, large employers (say, over 500 employees) could be required to offer and participate

in independent mediation services so that employees can receive a full explanation and can respond to the employer. Although nonbinding, mediation has a good record of tempering impulsive actions and reactions, and also can provide useful feedback. Large employers can also report their diversity profile at different levels of responsibility. Transparency will be a far more constructive incentive for a diverse workplace than legal fear causing employers to batten down the HR hatches.

People are "astonishingly unlike each other," Tocqueville noted. Hayek as well marveled at the "boundless variety of human nature—the wide range of differences in individual capacities and potentialities—is one of the most distinctive facts about the human species." All day long people of different temperaments and values will deal with others in ways that vary as much as the people themselves.

America is built on an abiding belief in the freedom of these unique individuals. That includes the ability to deal freely with other people, including the power to make judgments and the exposure to being judged. Liberating people to make these choices restores the role of character, which today is confined to the back lot of "subjective" values. It recalibrates the goals of the workplace—toward excellence and cooperation instead of entitlement. Candor replaces resentment.

People judging people is the currency of social interaction in a free society. Almost nothing we do is done alone. Our work, our play, our life in the neighborhood, our religious life, our connection to the political system all involve other people. This requires us to make judgments about them. We do this naturally, examining all facets of a person, and drawing on our sense of ethics, goodwill, likability, and effectiveness. Yes, it is true that these judgments also draw on feelings we don't respect, like racism or other stereotypes. It is important to protect against these tendencies, as I have discussed. But it is not possible, or desirable, to avoid making judgments about others. Without personal accountability, law will flood our lives and destroy honest interaction. Accountability is the price we pay for everyday freedom.

CHAPTER 7

RESPONSIBILITY IN WASHINGTON

n the 1970s a man from Sacramento named Pasquale Plescia took a bus to Washington to figure out why his Social Security checks were delayed and usually in the wrong amount. His story was picked up in the *Los Angeles Times*.

"I mean, this where the people are who run the show, right? . . . You ought to be able to get one little problem fixed up. . . . Well, I'll tell you something about this town. They've got a secret language here. You know that? Bureaucratese. Same thing we used to call double-talk. These government people, they don't hear you. They don't listen. You start to say something and they shut you out mentally, figuring they know right away what you're going to say before you say it.

"I knocked on doors here for two weeks but everyone's so busy with paperwork, they got no time for nothing else. I go to see one congressman—a priest, so I figure he's got humanitarian interests—and his aide says I've got to write him a letter first. . . . Another gives me a press release, and says, 'this is the Congressman's position on Social Security.' No kidding, that happened. So I go down to HEW [Department of Health,

Education, and Welfare]. They've got 130,000 people working for HEW, and you know what? They've got nobody to
make a complaint to."

Responsibility is a rare commodity in Washington. It's hard to
identify anyone who will actually accept the task of dealing with
your problem. Most businesses hire a lawyer who is a specialist in
the area and can guide them through the bureaucratic caves and
tunnels. Once the right official is located, however, chances are
he will open up the rulebook and say they can't do it for this or
that reason, unless you trudge through months or years of legal
processes. Social Security recently had a two-year backlog on disputes over disability payments, causing some recipients to sell their
homes to make ends meet while they waited.

Responsibility in government is even rarer at the highest levels
of public policy. Washington is on cruise control, just going in whatever direction it was headed toward yesterday, adjusted slightly in
response to daily headlines or special interest influence. Congress
has the job, for example, of making sure regulatory schemes enacted
in prior years actually deliver on the original goals. But it hasn't
fixed the well-known problems of special education laws. Nor does
Congress take responsibility for the future. Who is responsible for
the burgeoning national debt? I guess it's our children.

Congressmen look out their windows at the huge regulatory
edifice they've created over the years and throw up their hands.
Instead of tackling the problems caused by ineffective laws or
unforeseen circumstances, most seem to spend their days receiving constituents and special interests, acting as a complaint bureau
and dispensing largess to the well connected.

Washington presents a harder problem than anything I've
discussed so far. Some of the work required to restore our daily
freedoms can probably be done without restoring a culture of
responsibility to Washington; judges, for example, could start drawing the boundaries of lawsuits. We might even be able to mount

pressure to pass specific reforms, say, to overhaul special education laws. But many of the changes require major shifts in legal structure. Government must take a fresh look at how its laws work in practice, and what our society needs. That's what democracy is supposed to do. But that's not what's happening in Washington.

The disconnection between Washington and the rest of America has many causes, some inherent in the nature of government, some caused by our own unrealistic demands. But the mechanism by which government has slipped away from our democratic grasp is too much law. Law has replaced responsibility.

If teachers, doctors, managers, and the rest of us wade through law all day long, people in government are submerged in law. Officials are taught to comply with the rules and follow the process, not solve the problem in front of them. That's why the results are so often idiotic.

In response to Hurricane Katrina, FEMA went out and cornered the market on mobile homes and trailers, spending over $400 million for 19,000 units. Unfortunately, most of them could not be used because they did not comply with rules against mobile homes in floodplains. Instead of waiving the rules so that people could have places to live, they were stored at an abandoned airport in Hope, Arkansas. In 2007 a tornado in another part of Arkansas left 150 families homeless, and someone suggested sending some of the mobile homes to help out. This humane use of otherwise useless property was also blocked by a rule—FEMA could provide help only to places designated as a "federal disaster area." This is the government we've learned to hate—lurching here and there, like a badly designed robot, doing the wrong thing at the wrong time.

Detailed regulation is generally a formula for failure. The detail acts as a straitjacket, removing the authority to adapt to new circumstances and unintended consequences. The No Child Left Behind Law, for example, contains 670 pages of dictates, plus hundreds of pages of implementing rules by the Department of Education. The backfires can be heard across America. The requirement of "highly qualified" teachers, as seen earlier, often excludes good teachers while rewarding bad ones just because they went to graduate school. "Through the eyes of the people in Washington, DC I was unqualified." Jon Runnalls said after receiving the Montana Teacher of the Year in 2003. The sanctions for failure to meet "annual yearly progress" has prompted educators to put children across the land onto a kind of forced march on a testing treadmill. "Everything is test, test, test," bemoaned a teacher in Alaska. Officials in Washington charged with enforcing the law also see the inanities. But they don't have the power to alter these requirements of No Child Left Behind. It's the law.

There's hardly an area of society that isn't knocked off-balance by the unintended consequences of some inflexible regulatory scheme. Doctors and nurses go through the day negotiating a regulatory minefield. In 1996, for example, Congress passed HIPAA (Health Insurance Portability and Accountability Act), which includes provisions mandating privacy of patient information. Privacy seems like a worthy goal, but at what cost? Just the added bureaucracy for each patient adds over $1 billon to annual costs. That's the least of it. Self-consciousness about blurting out a patient's name is now added to other legal fears, as doctors worry about how to "talk to and about patients." Quality of care suffers as doctors will "no longer discuss treatments among themselves via email." Research on heart attack recovery at the University of Michigan slowed to a crawl when only one-third of the sample bothered to complete the necessary HIPAA paperwork.

Impairing open interaction among health care professionals inevitably leads to tragedy. In mental health, for example, a patient often can't make sensible judgments for himself. Yet because of HIPAA and other privacy laws, doctors and school officials feel unable to communicate to parents about a suicidal child. The right to privacy, like due process in schools, has taken a life of its own, supplanting the benefits of *in loco parentis* with a debilitating self-consciousness. Seung Hui Cho, the disturbed student who

killed thirty-four students at Virgina Tech in 2007, had a record of
frightening conduct that would have been of gravest concern to
both his parents and school administrators, but they weren't told
because of concerns about his right to privacy. What makes these
unintended consequences so frustrating is that medical privacy is
not exactly the big problem in America. Other than the general
principle of confidentiality (which existed before HIPAA), I suspect
most patients couldn't care less; HIPAA is just another variation of
the warnings that litter our daily landscape. Sign your name, sign
your name, sign your name, dutifully take the required copies, and
then sit down and wait for the doctor. "By now it likely has a shop-
ping list scrawled on it," one patient observed.

The failures of HIPAA, and No Child Left Behind, and hundreds
of other laws are not a secret to members of Congress; they hear
complaints all day long. But they don't feel they can do anything
about it. Fixing old laws requires the same process as passing new
ones. A congressman can't change the law, at least not without getting 217 colleagues and 60 senators together. An agency head can't
change the agency's own rules without going through a years-long
process of judicial review. The steady accretion of law and process
makes choices ever slower. "It used to take a few months for EPA
to set effluent guidelines for clean water," environmentalist Peter
Lehner observes. "Now the processes go on for years."

Washington has slowly sunk into an ocean of law, rules, and
processes, most created in the past forty years—over 100 million
words of binding federal statutes and rules, with more added every
year and almost none ever taken away. You may like the idea of
tight legal controls over bureaucrats—no official can do anything
without swimming through years of legal processes. But inertia
in government is costly. It's hard to change priorities, or fix what
doesn't work. The legal detail perpetuates failure while also insulating Washington from democratic accountability. Washington is
a veritable Atlantis, operating in its own strange ways for its own
goals, separated from the rest of America by fathoms of law.

Down in these depths of law, Washington has developed its own culture. There is a separate language, as Mr. Plescia discovered, with acronyms and phrases that are unintelligible except to those steeped in bureaucracy. Professor Ralph Hummel refers to these as "one directional words—words whose meaning is controlled by the speaker" and therefore not accessible to normal people. Washington operates toward different goals as well, focusing on appearance rather than accomplishment. One business leader, nominated for a subcabinet post by President Clinton, had this to say after getting caught up in a confirmation battle having nothing to do with his own conduct: "I'm an air-breathing animal and I somehow jumped into the deep end of the pool and I—I'm not able to grow gills fast enough. It's such a different environment."

A kind of rule stupor settles in. Professor Steven Kelman, who was in charge of procurement reform for Al Gore's reinventing government initiative, describes a contracting official who had been trained to try to be absolutely neutral among different bidders: "He told me proudly . . . about a bidder with whom the IRS had had terrible experience but [he] was careful not to tell anyone on the panel so as not to bias the evaluation process."

People in Washington like the culture of rules. All the law is a barrier to entry to outsiders. Rules appeal to the risk-averse side of human nature. Rules provide almost foolproof cover—who can blame you if you're following the rule? Rules relieve people of the need to think. All the law acts as a barrier to entry, insulating insiders from democratic accountability. They can relax in the caverns of rules instead of worrying about results. People are "mightily addicted to rules," the Scottish philosopher David Hume noted.

Periodic efforts to control government with more laws just make the problem worse. Trying to control bureaucracy usually creates more bureaucracy. Professor Paul Light calculated that there are now as many as thirty-two layers of federal officials between the person doing the job and the person on top. (The rule of thumb for well-run companies, by contrast, is five layers.) Laws designed to prevent corruption have the effect of thickening the cover of bureaucracy in which corruption can thrive. As Michael Reisman points out in his book on bribery reforms, "the very complexities and time-consumption factors introduced by a red-tape control system . . . create new incentives for bribes."

The problem is in the premise—that law should tell people how to do things. Making detailed laws is like pointing a car in one direction and leaving the passengers in it without the power to turn the wheel when they hit a curve. Sooner or later the car drives off a cliff. "Each fresh law," as the anarchist Peter Kropotkin wryly put it, is "a fresh miscalculation."

There was a time, at the beginning of modernism, when smart people thought that efficiency required treating people as mindless tools. Sociologist Max Weber bemoaned the antihuman aspects of systems where each person "is only a small cog in a ceaselessly moving mechanism" but thought that this was the price of efficiency: "Bureaucracy develops the more perfectly, the more it is 'dehumanized.'" Weber was wrong. Systems have their place, but a human is always the core.

For decades we have been working feverishly to create a legal regime that minimizes official flexibility—detailed rules, and then rules to explain the rules; open-ended rights, and then litigation to keep expanding the scope of the rights. America developed, historian Henry Steele Commager said, an "almost lawless passion for lawmaking." We succeeded in replacing human authority with law. Responsibility disappeared in an ocean of inflexible legal detail and uncontrollable rights.

It's hard to know when responsibility finally slipped out of sight in Washington. Legislators from the 1980s such as Howard Baker and Alan Simpson swear it has gotten far worse since then. But the bottom line is clear: Washington isn't doing its job. If the federal government were graded on its "annual yearly progress," as it demands of schools, funding would have been pulled long ago. Its worst feature is not ineptitude. Some agencies do their jobs well, and most muddle along, although usually in the wrong direction. Washington is far worse than inept—it is irresponsible.

Washington no longer cares about what's really needed in our society. It takes no responsibility for the future. It takes no responsibility for laws it has enacted in the past. It has taken a life of its own, pursuing goals that have little or nothing to do with the good of the country. In the depths of endless law and bureaucracy, the worst traits of politics have been allowed to fester, throwing off the unmistakable odor of greed and hypocrisy.

THE PROFILE OF AN IRRESPONSIBLE CULTURE

A couple of years ago I had a meeting with a Democratic leader in the House of Representatives to discuss better ways of handling medical malpractice disputes. A broad coalition of patient groups as well as providers had come together behind legislation that would authorize different pilot projects. Major editorial boards had endorsed the plan. There was (and still is) a crisis of confidence in health care justice. It's hard to object to a pilot project; why not see if something new might work better? This congressman said that it sounded like a constructive approach. Our dialogue then went as follows. "How do the trial lawyers feel about it?" "They hate it," I said. "Half the cost of medical malpractice goes to lawyers' fees." "We can't do it then," he said. "But the patient and consumer groups are for it," I reminded him. "Who do the trial lawyers supposedly represent?" "It doesn't matter," he said. "We can't support it if the lawyers are against it." End of meeting.

Not long after this, I met with a senior political adviser at the White House on the same subject. This would be a bipartisan breath of fresh air for President Bush, I argued. Just imagine the presidential press conference on the South Lawn with groups like AARP and former Democratic leaders like Bill Bradley supporting this initiative. This senior adviser acknowledged the political appeal of a bipartisan initiative but said that the president had decided to pursue a bill that would just put caps on medical damages, basically limiting pain and suffering damages awards. "But limiting damages won't restore trust that justice will get to the right decision," I argued. "Yes," he said, "I understand that. But that's what we're pushing. It's something the public can understand." So I asked what the odds were of damage caps actually getting enacted. He leaned back and reflected and said, "Oh, about one in a hundred." "That sounds right," I said, "so why doesn't the president try something that maybe has bipartisan support?" He then launched into a discussion about the "broader benefits" of advancing a bill that he knew wouldn't pass. I'm so naive that what he was saying didn't sink in until it was explained to me by junior staffers: The president was pushing a reform that he knew wouldn't pass—so that he could then blame the Democrats for not solving the problem.

I don't happen to believe in the death penalty, but these discussions tempt me to reconsider. It strikes me as a form of treason that senior officials in our democracy—one elected and one reporting directly to the president—view the crisis in health care as just another opportunity to make the other side look bad.

But this is business as usual in Washington. For years, for example, Democrats have been trying to get ratification of environmental treaties on POPs (persistent organic pollutants) and PICs (a requirement of "prior informed consent" before hazardous chemicals can be shipped). In 2007, after years of stalling, the Republicans finally announced a willingness to sign on. Now the Democrats refused to back it. Why? They didn't want the Republicans to look good on the environment. The Environmental Protection Agency has never been elevated to cabinet status, despite proposals to do so by both sides, because neither party wants it to occur while the other is in the White House.

Cynicism in politics is not new to our time. The challenge is to make it costly by holding the practitioners accountable. That's how we combat cheating and other vices. Competition in democracy is supposed to keep political leaders focused on serving the people, just as competition in the marketplace keeps large companies from becoming sluggish. But those democratic forces aren't working anymore. "[W]e have gradually developed governmental a institutions," economist Milton Friedman observed, "in which the people effectively have no voice." That's mainly because officials themselves have no voice. Democracy is paralyzed by its own inflexible laws and rules. Responsibility died through a form of democratic suicide—instead of self-immolation, it's self-immobilization.

Americans have pretty much given up on Washington. Even critics can't maintain their sense of outrage in the face of years of continuous frustration. Jonathan Rauch, a keen observer of special interests in Washington, recommends managing the ulterior motives as best we can. But the situation is not stable; the more we tolerate, the worse it gets. The growing cynicism about Washington by the citizenry ironically makes it easier for insiders to be openly cynical. "Yes, isn't it terrible how partisan things have gotten . . . but that's the way it is." Winks and nods become explicit. Just as bureaucrats follow rules instead of trying to achieve goals, politicians play politics all day long.

Washington has become a land of political make-believe. The point is not governing but winning. Success is measured not by policy improvements but by how many political traps you've set to embarrass the other side. Posturing is the main activity. Members of Congress hold hearings on scandals or other matters of public interest so that they can give campaign speeches on camera that typically play to their "base" of supporters. Hearings on steroid use in professional sports, for example, don't have much to do with public policy. So prevalent is the practice of speaking just to have a highlight reel that most speeches on the House or Senate floor are given to an empty chamber. Their congressional colleagues know that nothing important is being said. "We used to fight hard in the campaigns, and things could get rough," former Senator Howard Baker observed, "but once we were in office we worked together to govern. Now the campaigning never stops."

The constituents in Washington are not mainly the folks back home; a little pork and constituent service will usually take care of them. The important constituents are the special interests that provide the resources for political campaigns. Interest groups have extensive mailing lists that can be used to support or oppose candidates and issues. Unions can turn out thousands of campaign workers. Wall Street firms can fill a room with people each giving the legal maximum. In an age of campaign finance regulation, with limits on contributions, special interests can effectively bundle hundreds or thousands of separate supporters.

In return, special interests ask only one thing: The political leader must look out for their particular cause. What that usually boils down to is preventing any change. The most powerful interests have only one issue. The trial lawyers care only about preventing any legislation that curbs lawsuits. The National Rifle Association has only one mission—preventing legislation that limits gun ownership. Groups like these focus all their resources on preventing change. Intense pressure, almost unimaginably relentless pressure, will be concentrated on any politician or regulator who even considers some unwanted change in law. The phone will be ringing off the hook with big contributors, best friends, large employers, all somehow now devoted to preventing any change. Once you get in the grips of one of these groups, it's almost impossible to get away. Breaking ranks from a special interest is like trying to leave an organized crime family—it doesn't just lose their support. You become the target of their fury. Senator Jay Rockefeller learned the hard way when he tried to champion legal reform in the late 1990s. "He'll never make that mistake again," one staffer told me.

Just as bureaucracy has its own language, the political rhetoric of Washington can be decoded into special interest obligations. Most Democratic politicians I know believe that lawsuits have gotten out of hand. But they would never say it publicly because that would offend the trial lawyers, the party's second-largest source of campaign funds. Instead politicians stand up, without so much as a blush, and deliver self-righteous speeches about preserving the "right to sue." The hypocrisy is sometimes breathtaking. Republican candidates who spent their entire careers as pro-choice all of sudden believe in the right to life when running for president. Democrats who supported the North American Free Trade Agreement (NAFTA) make overturning it the focus of their campaign rhetoric, at least in states with high unemployment.

Most special interests are not evil or venal. They represent legitimate constituencies that are important to the fabric of our society—for example, the American Medical Association, the Chamber of Commerce, and the Sierra Club. You would think that they might join together for reforms that benefit all society. But most interest groups, like politicians, are tied to their "base" and do not venture beyond a narrow agenda of self-protection. Medical associations stubbornly resist any effort at regulatory oversight over doctors, for example, even though that might make it easier for them to achieve other legislative goals. Environmental groups oppose any push for nuclear power—so, by default, power companies meet demand by burning more fossil fuel. "Many interest groups would rather push their point of view and lose," observed Rod DeArment, former chief of staff to Senator Bob Dole, "than go out on a limb by negotiating a compromise."

As long as there has been organized government, people have tried to manipulate it for their own purposes. Kings were surrounded by sycophants. Abraham Lincoln was surrounded by job seekers. President Garfield was assassinated by a campaign worker disappointed that he hadn't gotten the job he deserved. Our founders knew that government was a magnet for self-seekers, but thought, as Madison wrote in *The Federalist Papers*, that these "factions" would neutralize each other, and that the general interest would emerge in a competition. But Madison proved incorrect. There's no competition for the greater good—there's an exhausting queue of group after group demanding pounds of flesh from the common weal.

Special interests do not run Congress, at least not in the sense of directing public goals—they could never agree on priorities for running the country. Indeed, other than tax exemptions or pork barrel favors, special interests rarely succeed at getting favorable legislation. But they have a hammerlock on the status quo. Passing a law is hard enough in the best of circumstances. Now think about herding all those congressional cats together to amend what's wrong with a law—who will get headlines for that thankless task? Then some special interest puts its boot on your neck to protect a legal provision that it considers an entitlement. That's why, once a law is enacted, it acquires an almost invincible stature. Repairing No Child Left Behind, for example, is sure to offend schools of education, which want to keep teachers going to grad school to be certified as "highly qualified." Just raising the idea of reforming special education will trigger an explosion. Special ed advocates don't focus on abuses of the system—they want to preserve as many rights as possible. That's how they see their job, and they'll chain themselves to the senator's desk, screaming all day, to keep those entitlements.

Special interests sometimes come to dominate the goals of agencies, as the defunct Interstate Commerce Commission used to protect the trucking industry. But the phenomenon of agency "capture"—where the foxes take over the henhouse—is overblown, in my view. Many agencies are confronted with conflicting interests—for example, the tension between cable operators and telephone companies at the Federal Communications Commission—and the agency has to make a choice. What special interest groups can do with agencies is prevent them from acting, either by inundating them under expert reports or, more efficiently, by just calling up Congress. At one point in the 1990s the Occupational Safety and Health Administration wanted to issue guidelines—not even enforceable rules—on how better to protect clerks at convenience stores from crime. "I received 128 letters from members of Congress expressing outrage that I would even consider such a thing," Joe Dear, the former head of OSHA, observed, "all put up to it by the convenience store association. The proposal was dead on arrival."

It is hard to overestimate the power of the status quo in Washington. Farm subsidies were originally enacted in 1933 to relieve the suffering of farmers, who then constituted 25 percent of the population. Today farmers constitute only 2 percent of the population and have incomes higher than the national average. Yet seventy-five years later the farm subsidy continues. Even more illogically, the subsidy is awarded to only a certain category of large farmers, basically growers of corn, sugarcane, and wheat and other grains. Many of these farms are corporate enterprises.

Almost no one outside Congress defends this subsidy. Why is it fair to subsidize large sugar and grain combines while leaving out those who grow fruits and vegetables? By driving up production, the subsidies drive down prices and make it hard for farmers in the third world to compete in world markets. Government subsidies also violate our obligations under a host of free trade treaties. Why do we want to give $10 billion in taxpayer money to rich farmers? Aren't there better ways to use the money? That's enough money to provide health insurance for three million people.

No one can kill the farm bill, however, because the large corporate farmers have the undivided loyalty of midwestern legislators who will do anything, it seems, to preserve this flow of government largess. Other legislators need the votes of these midwestern representatives for their own pet interests, so year after year they hold their noses and vote for the farm bill. "If government waste were an art form," columnist Robert Samuelson observed, "the farm bill is the Mona Lisa."

The harm caused by special interests is not mainly pork barrel abuses—that at least has quantifiable limits—but the inability to govern. The special interests circle overhead, ready to swoop down at the earliest hint of change. Members of Congress know where it's safe—the status quo. The pattern of modern politics is all too clear:

Talk about reform in campaigns, and then do nothing. Reforms that affect the powerful interests—improving legal reliability, reining in entitlements, holding public employees accountable—are not seriously considered. That's why neither of the officials I spoke with had any interest in pursuing medical liability pilot projects. They know that change is almost impossible. This is Washington.

The public sees the inaction and self-interested grandstanding, but doesn't know what to do about it. The longer this continues, the harder it is to fix—acting responsibly means owning up to hard choices and overdue debts. I had a long discussion one day with a senior Republican senator about how polarized and self-interested politics had become. He frankly admitted, "We don't know how to break out of this rut."

Every major political figure in the past thirty years has vowed to curb special interest power and get Washington back on track to serve the public. In his "malaise speech," Jimmy Carter said:

> Washington . . . seems incapable of action. You see a Congress twisted and pulled in every direction by hundreds of well-financed and powerful special interests. You see every extreme position defended to the last vote, almost to the last breath by one unyielding group or another.

Similar sentiments have been echoed since then by Ronald Reagan: "Our concern must be for a special interest group that has been too long neglected. . . . They are in short, 'We the People' "; George H. W. Bush: "The time has come to put the national interest ahead of the special interest"; Bill Clinton: "I know that facing up to these interests will require courage"; Newt Gingrich: "Elected officials have become so entrenched and protected that they are unresponsive to the public they were elected to serve"; and George W. Bush: "The federal budget has too many special interest projects." Through all these administrations, Washington has only sunk deeper into the swamp of bureaucracy and special interests.

What's needed is not a Herculean push to fix this law or that. We could spend ten lifetimes doing combat with special interests to fix all the lousy laws on the books. What we need to do is abandon the system. We must walk away from the heavy weight of accumulated laws, each in the grip of special interests, and create anew a government focused on goals and personal accountability.

REWRITING WASHINGTON

When institutions lose their sense of purpose, the only solution is to shake them up and start afresh. "A little rebellion now and then is a good thing," Jefferson wrote to Madison in 1787, "and as necessary in the political world as storms are in the physical. . . . It is a medicine for the sound health of government."

To implement the programs of the New Deal, FDR basically gave up on existing agencies and instead created more than sixty new departments. The Civilian Conservation Corps, the program to organize the unemployed to build public works, was authorized by a statute that was barely five pages long, delegating authority to a director and providing funding. Three months later, over 250,000 Americans were employed. *Washington Monthly* founder Charles Peters, an astute observer of bureaucratic failure, recalled the excitement of working in the early days at the founding of the Peace Corps: "We had no rules. We ran around in our socks figuring out how to get this going, and, by God, we did it."

Government today is organized to minimize official discretion. Friedrich Hayek, no advocate of big government, observed that America no longer had a government "*under* law" but a government shackled by countless legislative mandates—instead of general rules, statutes became mere "directions." Without freedom by officials to take responsibility, government lost the ability to account for "the immeasurable multitude of particular facts which must determine the order of its activities."

Absent a powerful intervention, creating a new model of governance, the culture of Washington will not change. "Our system of managing in the public sector," Professor Steven Kelman concludes, "may rob the people in it of their faculties to such an extent that, like a person on a mind-numbing drug, they no longer even realize that they are missing anything."

America needs to rewrite its legal and regulatory codes. Bulldozing is not too strong a term. Most of the laws and rules long ago lost their connection to real problems and real people. They exist not because they do the job but because . . . well, because someone once took the trouble to write them. Our political leaders might as well be security guards in an archive of failed ideas—detail for its own sake, processes designed to remove responsibility, elaborate logical constructions to reconcile unnecessary prior logic. The HIPAA rules governing medical privacy, for example, presume that any disclosure is invalid unless it satisfies enumerated bureaucratic criteria. Doctors can't internalize the regulatory jargon, and so many, perhaps most, have no idea where the boundaries are.

The first organizing principle of government should be to have clear goals, and to designate persons to take responsibility to accomplish those goals. For democracy to function, we must have a direct line between our public goals and responsible officials in Washington.

Responsibility in turn requires giving officials the authority needed to do the job. Law must set boundaries to establish the goals and powers of the responsible official—otherwise the power is arbitrary. But the boundaries must also leave ample room for flexibility—otherwise the bureaucratic rigidity will force solutions that make no sense. Perhaps the most important function of boundaries is to provide a clear hierarchy of accountability—that's how we keep officials honest.

The second organizing principle of government, helping to keep officials focused on public goals, is that law should consist (generally) of general principles. The Constitution, a document that occupies barely ten pages in the United States Code, refers to "life, liberty or property" without trying to define exactly what that means. The common law that we inherited from England consists of general principles, such as the standard of behavior "to behave as a reasonable person would in the circumstances." In both cases, the principles are given life by judges. The Uniform Commercial Code, which governs most contractual arrangements, sets protocols for contractual arrangements, but ultimately also hinges on obligations of "commercial reasonableness" and "good faith."

Law based on general principles marries legal goals with personal responsibility. Principles are comprehensible because they state an aspiration—say, reasonable care for the disabled. Principles are adaptable—as a result, there is an opportunity by the responsible official to balance competing circumstances. Principles offer more consistency, studies show, than the supposedly uniform "command and control" dictates—this paradox is explained by the leveling influence of common sense. The most important virtue of law based on principles is that it allows us to judge officials by their actual results—not by compliance with rules. Detailed rules have their place, especially where uniform protocols are needed—say, speed limits or building codes. Guidelines can also be useful, but as with criminal sentencing, there must be room for flexibility to account for the circumstances. Principles are alive. Rules ossify.

Our founding fathers recognized both the impulse and the mistake of Congress's trying to dictate actions by officials. The discretionary power of the government officials was a hotly debated point at the Constitutional Convention. Some feared that the executive would run amok. But others, led by Alexander Hamilton, prevailed with the argument that individual responsibility not only is the practical way to get things done but is also the safest course because it permits accountability.

Within weeks after George Washington was inaugurated in 1789, the issue came to a head again: Did the president have the power to remove officials without congressional approval? In the debates in Congress, James Madison restated why locating responsibility in the executive was essential to accountability:

> It is one of the most prominent features of the Constitution, a principle that pervades the whole system, that there should be the highest possible degree of responsibility in all the Executive officers thereof; any thing, therefore, which tends to lessen this responsibility, is contrary to its spirit and intention. * * * If the President should possess alone the power of removal from office, those who are employed in the execution of law will be in their proper situation, and the chain of dependence be preserved; the lowest officers, and the middle grade, and the highest, will depend, as they ought, on the President, and the President on the community. . . .

The early days of the Republic showed that administrative discretion was unavoidable in almost every regulatory and fiscal activity. Whether property should be forfeited for failure to pay tariff duties, for example, was a decision that could be subject to judicial review but could hardly be laid out in statutory form. As Hamilton put it, this was "a power of too much delicacy and importance to be determined otherwise than upon mature deliberation." Hamilton was an unabashed advocate of executive power, but even modern philosophers skeptical of regulatory power acknowledge that responsible government necessarily involves human choice, not rote compliance. "At every stage of the governmental hierarchy," Hayek observed, "considerable discretion must be granted to the subordinate agencies."

Undertaking this project to radically simplify federal law would certainly shake things up in Washington. But the goal, in truth, is pretty unrevolutionary—to let government accomplish its goals. Restoring personal responsibility is hardly a new idea—it's the only way anything works. Look at any successful government agency or program, and you will find officials who, with or without authorirization, take personal initiative to meet the public goals. At the Securities and Exchange Commission, for example, every public offering of securities is reviewed by an SEC official, who gives comments to the issuer and then engages in a back-and-forth to work out differences in view. This process between lawyers generally results in sound disclosure. The SEC has the advantage of operating under statutes that are relatively spare, affording officials the flexibility to deal with unique situations as they occur day to day.

The antitrust prohibitions against monopolization and price-fixing, enacted in the trust-busting era of Theodore Roosevelt, are contained in a grand total of two paragraphs. The record of the antitrust agencies (the Antitrust Division of the Department of Justice and the Federal Trade Commission) is a little more controversial than the SEC's, but few people doubt the integrity of the agencies or their independence from special interests.

With a little leadership, even rule-bound agencies can break free and advance toward public goals. In *The Death of Common Sense*, I was highly critical of OSHA. Inspectors would visit factories and issue scores of violations for infractions that had nothing to do with safety, like having railings that were 41 inches high instead of the required 42 inches, or not posting a hazardous substance form on how to use Windex. As part of Al Gore's reinventing government initiative, however, OSHA undertook to reform itself. A regional administrator in Maine, Bill Freeman, invented a program that replaced "gotcha" inspections with voluntary safety plans, devised by employers in conjunction with OSHA, that focused on actual safety instead of rule compliance. When Al Gore tried to scale it up nationwide, the plan didn't work as well; success seemed to hinge on Freeman's relationship with the Maine business community. But Gore's goal changed the agency's mind-set. OSHA administrator Joe Dear devised another program, focusing on accident rates industry by industry. When a safety analyst at OSHA noticed a spike in accidents in home building, an OSHA director worked with the Home Builders' Association to develop a program that reduced those accidents. Focusing on the goal of safety, not the rules, was the key to effectiveness.

The power of government scares us, as it did our founders. But history has proved that Madison was correct—the best safeguard is to shine a bright light on the individual with responsibility. Prosecutors, for example, hold more power than anyone. Criminal laws are written in such a way that, as one judge said, you "can indict a ham sandwich." But people aren't usually sent up the river for minor infractions, because prosecutors generally exercise their discretion in a way that passes the smell test of reasonable fairness. Prosecutors don't abuse their power because we know who the prosecutor is, and we can see whom he is indicting. The occasional prosecutorial scandals—for example, the rogue prosecutor who manufactured evidence to indict the Duke lacrosse players in 2006—only underscore how relatively well prosecutors use their power most of the time.

There's a myth that detailed rules give us more control over officials. That's what motivates Congress to write statutes hundreds of pages long and inspires conservatives and liberals alike to demand legal instructions for every official choice. But misconduct is far easier in a rule-bound system. As exhibit A, just look at Jack Abramoff's schemes and other recent scandals in Washington. A rule-bound culture allows bad people to hide, while good people lose their grasp on right and wrong. "By declaring war on elitism," Fareed Zakaria observes in *The Future of Freedom*, "we have produced politics by a hidden elite, unaccountable, unresponsive and often unconcerned with any larger public interest." Dictators know that the best way to subjugate a population is to wrap their power in the trappings of legal regularity. Hannah Arendt famously described the "banality of evil"—in supervising the murder of millions, Eichmann was just following orders.

Broad principles, by contrast, allow accountability based on results and, far from allowing officials unfettered discretion, serve as boundaries that hem in discretion. Justice Cardozo explained how it works in a judicial context. The judge "is not a knight-errant roaming at will. . . . He is to draw his inspiration from consecrated principles . . . informed by tradition, methodized by analogy." Public goals and legal principles provide a far more effective basis for accountability than rote compliance.

Washington must scrape away decades of encrusted law to reconnect the chains of accountability essential in our democracy. Area by area, laws should be replaced by simpler statutes that set goals, allocate funding, and give responsibility to identifiable officials. The goals of No Child Left Behind, for example, could far better be advanced by a statute written in a few dozen pages, setting goals for national testing, and giving officials flexibility to see what kind of testing regime works. The privacy goals of HIPAA could satisfactorily be met by a few protocols for using electronic records and a general principle of confidentiality—"Patient records shall be kept confidential and used only for legitimate purposes"—without a requirement of paperwork and without fear of lawsuits. We want doctors and nurses to think about our health, not be preoccupied by what they can or cannot say out loud.

This will not come easily. The special interests won't like it. Probably no one in Washington will like it. That's why Washington won't do it. The modern record of Washington on reforms like this is perfect: it has a batting average of zero. But that doesn't mean it can't be done.

TAKING RESPONSIBILITY OURSELVES

Washington can only be fixed from the outside. Outside pressure is how all institutions stay healthy. Without fierce competition large companies avoid tough choices needed for long-term survival. Municipal services tend to work reasonably well when the public sees the effects of their success or failure immediately—garbage collection comes to mind—and there are identifiable officials, the sanitation commissioner and the mayor, who catch holy hell if the trash starts piling up.

Partisan politics was supposed to provide competition for the greater good, but instead it's become a race to the bottom. The few reform ideas that actually make it into law tend to fail because, as with No Child Left Behind, they pile layers of legal concrete onto educators already crushed by law. Other than Al Gore's reinventing government program, I can think of almost no reforms that actually increased responsibility for officials.

Accountability in the traditional sense is not sufficient, however. Removing the immunity of civil servants from accountability about job performance, as occurred in Georgia, is certainly essential— otherwise Congress and the president can pretend they have no authority over how laws are implemented. But that won't liberate officials from the bureaucratic concrete. Other suggestions along these lines would have only modest impact. Term limits in Congress would achieve some turnover from time to time but would do nothing to improve accountability when in office. Ballot initiatives can produce change in a particular state, as in California, but getting them passed requires a crusade, and the resulting laws are almost impossible to amend.

Starting over is probably not practical. I had a fantasy once about moving the national capital somewhere else. We'd get an entirely fresh group of public servants, because the current crew would be stuck in Washington, unable to sell their homes. Who would buy houses in a place with no jobs? Once the new government had settled in someplace else, say, St. Louis, we could give a concession to Disney to run Washington as a theme park on condition that it hire everyone there to do exactly what they were doing before—pretending to do something.

But the problem, in truth, is not mainly the people. There are lots of good people in Washington. But they work in a culture that has lost its capacity to take responsibility. The challenge is how to lead a turnaround of a government whose main flaw is that it can never turn around.

There's only one way to pry Washington loose from the status quo. Because Washington will never do what's right, people outside Washington have to assume this leadership. We must form a national coalition of citizen leaders to propose an overhaul of government. I'm not sure this has occurred on a national level, at least not since the days of Tom Paine and Samuel Adams. This may seem indirect, and let me admit that I come to this conclusion only because I see no other way. Once it gets over the hurdle of public credibility, however, a civic coalition led by people of influence can build pressure for changes of almost any scope.

The organizing model is a shadow government. Instead of partisan opposition, this shadow government would be run by citizens who, eschewing official position, develop legislative proposals in the areas most in need of change. Someone must do the hard work, for example, of sorting out the mess in health care. As one Democratic congressman told a group of health care experts, "Congress will never be able to bring all these pieces together. You have to work it out among yourselves and bring us the proposal." Think of the base-closing commissions active in the 1990s—independent committees designated by Congress to recommend which military bases should be shut down and instituted precisely to avoid congressional gridlock.

What's needed here is not to seize power, but to fill the vacuum of moral authority. Ancient Romans distinguished between people with power, such as an army general, and people with authority, who were respected for their wisdom and, often, their lack of self-interest. People with authority command not troops but the trust of others and, as a result, are often more influential in matters of gravity. "The favor of the sovereign may confer power," Gibbon observed, but "the esteem of the people can alone bestow authority."

The lever is public opinion. There's no stronger force in society. "There is an amazing strength," Tocqueville observed, "in the expression of the will of a whole people." This was true even in the days of kings, and is especially true in a democratic state. Public opinion is amorphous yet unmistakable—reflected in the way people talk about issues, and in the frame of reference of the media. To be a force for change, public opinion must congeal into specific ideas; a general malaise is not enough. When it does, as Thomas Jefferson wrote to Lafayette, "the force of public opinion cannot be resisted." The dictator of Romania Nicolae Ceauşescu was speaking to a huge assembly in 1989 when, in a pause, someone shouted, "Down with the dictator." Another shouted, "Timisoara," the site of recent brutal atrocities. The crowd picked up the chants, and Ceauşescu fled from the stage. After decades of tyranny, the rebellion took only days.

Mobilizing public opinion into a change agenda requires an orchestrated campaign. Sometimes this results in a movement, led by one or more people—notably, Martin Luther King, Jr., to end segregation. But sometimes there is a successful campaign with neither a broad movement nor identifiable leaders—say, the campaign to reduce smoking. Either way, once a campaign picks up steam, political leaders won't resist. Politicians are lagging indicators, and will blow with the wind. What's different about this campaign is that the target is not a specific evil, such as racism or smoking, but Washington itself.

Finding leaders who do not aspire to official power is an essential asset, because it enhances credibility. Al Gore is far more credible as an advocate against global warming because he's not running for office. Former political leaders like Bill Bradley, Jeb Bush, Mario Cuomo, Newt Gingrich, Tom Kean, and Bob Kerrey, and municipal leaders such as Mike Bloomberg, Shirley Franklin, and Richard Daley, are perfect candidates to help lead this effort. Retired leaders of business and universities also have experience in forging coalitions and making tough choices.

A shadow government run by citizen leaders may be a new idea, but most communities have civic groups that, although lacking official power, have enormous sway over local affairs. A few examples: The Civic Committee in Chicago, comprised of leading citizens from all sectors, is deeply involved in almost all issues of public importance, from rebuilding airports to school reform. In the 1980s a few New Yorkers concerned about the deterioration of Central Park in New York came up with a plan to take it over—creating a group to design a complete overhaul, organize ongoing maintenance, and raise private funds to supplement the public budget—and Central Park is now a jewel. In Kentucky, a former governor, Bert T. Combs, teamed up with former New Dealer Ed Pritchard to lead a successful campaign to require equalization of school funding across the state. I've been involved in civic activities in New York my entire adult life and have witnessed dozens of public projects in which private citizens took the initiative and turned the tide—for example, saving Grand Central Terminal, under the leadership of Jacqueline Kennedy Onassis, writer Brendan Gill, and preservationist Kent Barwick. Another was changing the zoning code so the lights and billboards on Times Square wouldn't disappear as office buildings started being developed there. At Common Good, we've been able to develop proposals for change supported by both teachers' unions and boards of education, by patient groups and health care providers.

Everyone knows the system is broken. People long for genuine leadership. We should stop looking to Washington to fix itself and come up with solutions ourselves. This is not utopian—it's a campaign, like any other, requiring money, staff, and conflict. As sure as the sun rises, a group with money and clout will attract political champions. Sooner or later, if the proposals are practical, they will become law. Like a dead limb, the rigid inertia of Washington will break when any credible force is applied to it.

Rewriting law, history shows, can energize an entire society. In ancient Rome, the emperor Justinian was famous for taking "the vast mass of juristic writings which served only to obscure the law" and rewriting them in a coherent code. In Justinian's time, similar to ours, the "mania for juristic writing was a kind of cancer." His code of uniform principles represented a clean break from the legal past and served as the legal foundation for Europe for centuries. Napoleon did the same thing with what is now called the Napoleonic Code, uniform general principles setting the legal boundaries for social interaction. Napoleon considered this new code his finest accomplishment. "The Revolution had turned the French into so many grains of sand," Napoleon believed, and his new code, written by four distinguished jurists, would "throw upon the soil of France a few blocks of granite to give a direction to the public spirit." The Napoleonic Code still acts as the foundation for legal systems in much of Western Europe (and in Louisiana). On a more modest level, the American Law Institute was formed in the 1920s for the explicit purpose of restating coherent principles out of the thousands of judicial decisions that had accumulated since the founding of the Republic. The ALI's Restatements of the Law, periodically updated, have not been adopted by legislatures. But they are considered authoritative by all courts and therefore might as well be law. The Restatements remain the bedrock of common law jurisprudence.

Washington needs a dramatic legal overhaul on the same order as these historic reforms. I don't want to understate the organizational challenge here. We don't have (or want) Napoleon telling us what to do. Creating this new civic authority requires organizing a respected group of citizen leaders; developing specific proposals; working with the public to fine-tune the proposals; campaigning for public approval; and putting pressure on Washington to adopt the proposals. This once-in-a-century challenge will likely take a decade or longer.

Ambitious though this may be, it's a lot less daunting than what our founding fathers faced: getting people to agree to revolt; fighting a war of independence; forming a union that didn't work (the

Articles of Confederation); coming together again in a constitutional convention to hammer out a new model of governance; selling this to the public (*The Federalist Papers*); and then doing the hard work of governing.

America doesn't need a new Constitution, just a healthy spring cleaning and a practical approach to making public choices without crushing us under endless law. We don't even need to change public goals (although the farm bill might finally disappear). The main change in Washington is to restore room so that officials can focus on our public goals, not mindless compliance, and we can identify whom to blame when things don't work. The goal is for Washington to be an open field rather than an overgrown swamp, with the field bounded by public goals, legal principles, and mechanisms for personal accountability. In an open structure, Congress could start exercising oversight over how laws actually function. This would be the most radical change of all: Congress actually taking responsibility.

CHAPTER 8

THE FREEDOM TO MAKE A
DIFFERENCE

A t lunch one day with a close friend, a respected journalist, I mentioned that a broad coalition had come together behind the idea of creating expert health courts. By making justice reliable, I explained, doctors would no longer have the incentive to squander billions in defensive medicine. With an expert court that could sort through the complexities of medical judgment, doctors would feel more comfortable being open about uncertainties and errors. Patients injured by mistakes would get paid more quickly and reliably.

Eyes flashing, she interrupted. "Who would guarantee that these judges weren't in the doctors' pockets?" I suggested that the judges could be appointed through a neutral screening panel. The retort was immediate: "Who will appoint the screening panel?" Reputation and professional character should stand for something, I suggested. After all, we can't abdicate responsibility just because that involves the exercise of human judgment. As I talked, the journalist—remember, this is a friend—looked at me as if I'd been caught cheating.

There's a lot going on in that little exchange. The distrust of authority is palpable. The core assumption is that society can be organized without human intervention. The idea of a judge making legal rulings on standards of care struck her as an invitation to abuse, a form of tyranny instead of a key ingredient of the rule of law.

This is the mind-set of our time. No idea is more unpalatable to the modern mind than giving someone authority to make choices that affect other people. That's why we have law, or so we believe—to dictate or oversee almost any life activity. Law, we think, should protect people from the judgment of others.

Our fears of human authority are hardly irrational, particularly in an anonymous, interdependent society. Decisions by judges and officials affect our lives in countless ways—the air we breathe, the scope of our health care, the fairness of justice, our careers, the success of our schools, and the safety of toys. Who are these people? They can do their jobs well, or poorly. A judge can be fair, or one-sided. Perhaps it is natural that we want a thick covering of law to insulate us from their choices and, just in case, a legal self-help kit if some decision emerges that we don't like.

Now that we have forty years of experience with this expansive concept of law, however, we can safely conclude that it wasn't a good innovation. The goal was to protect against unfair authority, but the effect was to preclude fair authority. As an unintended part of the bargain, we lost much of our freedom.

A crowded society can't operate unless officials have the authority to make common choices—drawing the boundaries of lawsuits, for example, and maintaining order in the classroom. Our freedom depends on these choices—to allow our children to focus on learning, and to let us go through the day without walking on eggshells. The people making these choices are not the enemy, but our surrogates. Many of them are the people next door—teachers, principals, counselors, ministers, nurses, doctors, managers, foremen, and inspectors, as well as public officials and judges. We need them to do their best, not be paralyzed by law.

There's a lot of talk about the decline of leadership in our society. America lacks leaders not because of a genetic flaw in our generation, at least not one that anyone has discovered. We lack leaders because we've basically made leadership unlawful. America doesn't even allow a teacher to run a classroom, or a judge to dismiss a $54 million claim for a lost pair of pants. Washington is legally dead, unable to breathe any sense into outmoded laws, and unable to prevent special interests from feeding off its carcass.

Social commentators also note the decline in civic involvement. Robert Bellah finds that freedom has been redefined—instead of the power to make a difference, Americans increasingly view freedom as the right to be left alone. Robert Putnam in *Bowling Alone* talks about the loss of "social capital" when people no longer participate in community activities. Apathy in America is not our natural state, however. It too is caused, at least in part, by a sense of powerlessness. What good are the parents' ideas if the bureaucracy prevents the principal from acting on them? Why bother to get involved in politics when nothing sensible seems possible? "Each individual feels helpless to affect anything beyond the immediate environment," Professor Warren Bennis observes, "and so retreats into an ever-contracting private world."

Law is supposed to be a structure that promotes our freedom. It does this by setting boundaries that define an open field of freedom. Instead law has moved in on daily life, becoming the arbiter of potentially every disagreement in a free society. We've asked law to do too much—trying to enforce fairness in daily relations is not freedom, but a form of utopia that predictably degenerates into squealing demands for me, me, me.

We need to snap out of our legal trance. Freedom is not defined by fairness—that's hopeless, because everyone has a different view, usually tilted toward himself. Freedom is defined by outside boundaries of what is legally unfair. There's a difference: Setting outer boundaries allows people to make free choices, whether it's running the classroom, managing the department, or putting an arm around a crying child. Bring law into daily disagreements, and you might as well give a legal club to the most unreasonable and selfish person in the enterprise.

The dream was to create a legal system that was self-executing and no longer subject to racism and other societal abuses. The goal was understandable. But law is only a tool, made by humans and only as good as the humans who are using it. Law can't make any final decisions, at least not without unleashing all the idiocies of central planning. For anything to work properly (including law), humans on the spot must make choices.

Still, you might say, legal process can make people justify the fairness of their decisions. That's what due process is all about, putting government to the proof before it takes away our "life, liberty or property." Why not use due process to guarantee fairness throughout society? That's what we've been told is innovative about modern law—make people in authority justify their choices to whoever's affected. Typically American, we think we can have it all. Let's have law everywhere and freedom too. Of course teachers, counselors, officials, and others can make decisions. They just need to justify their decisions in a legal proceeding.

Justification is now part of our daily culture. We demand it of others and expect it of ourselves. You'd better not make a decision that affects someone unless you're prepared to justify why it's fair.

But most decisions, although readily second-guessed by someone else, can rarely be justified in a legal sense. How do you prove that $54 million is an absurd amount for a pair of pants? It just is. How do you prove that sending Johnny home for misbehavior is fair? Well, I'm the principal here, and I know Johnny, and I think it's fair. People just have to decide. These judgments can be wrong or unfair, and that's why we can give others the authority to overrule these decisions. But rarely can people *prove* the wisdom or fairness of their choices in any objective way.

The confusion of good judgment with legal proof may be the most insidious fallacy of modern law. Due process was not designed as a litmus test for good judgment—it was designed as a high hurdle that the state had to cross before taking away a citizen's life, liberty, or property. We shouldn't be surprised that expanding due process to daily choices discourages the choices needed to get through the day. Putting daily decisions through the legal wringer does not make the decisions better. It gives us parents who make legal threats over bad grades, and officials who put handcuffs on five-year-olds.

The overlay of law destroys the human instinct needed to get things done. Accomplishment is personal. Anyone who has felt the pride of a job well done knows this. The power of freedom, as well as the joy of personal fulfillment, comes from spontaneity and invention, not logic and proof. Somehow we must learn to appreciate again the complexity of human judgment, and redirect our fears toward making our own judgments about people and their decisions, not trying to come up with a system that is better than mere mortals.

HOW LAW UNDERMINES GOOD JUDGMENT

Societies operate under preconceptions that are rarely expressed but are implicit in everything that we do. The reflexive distrust by my journalist friend is a fair warning that what I'm saying disrupts some deeply felt preconception. The radical idea here is this: Right and wrong can't be programmed or proved. It's always a matter of personal judgment. Modern societies have been organized on the incorrect premise, as Vaclav Havel observes, that "the world . . . is a wholly knowable system, governed by a finite number of universal laws that man can grasp—objectively describing, explaining and controlling everything."

The quest for objective truth is not merely futile, however. It is actively destructive of good judgment. People who feel they must demonstrate the correctness of decisions, studies have repeatedly shown, will make worse decisions. This seems counterintuitive, I know. It's hard to argue with the logic of more logic. But trying to take judgment apart into logical parts—the main goal of modern legal process—usually ends up ruining it. This is particularly true with everyday choices. Choices readily justified are those with a logic that can be replayed with objective facts. "I followed the rule." "I ordered the extra test." People start going through the day looking for objective markers that they can point to. What can I do to demonstrate that this was the right or fair thing to do? Pretty soon the quest for logic leads people to some irrelevant place, far away from the real world of accomplishment.

What modern law fails to appreciate is that judgment is only partially conscious. "Amazingly few people," management expert Peter Drucker observed, "know how they get things done." Humans often act brilliantly without knowing why. This shouldn't come as a surprise. Humans, like other living things, have capabilities that are hard-wired into our genetic code. Bees are good at making honey, and tigers effective at stalking their prey, but neither could sit on the witness stand and explain how they do it.

Humans have a kind of gyroscope that allows them to lean this way and that to get to their goals without ever comprehending exactly why choices were made. The gyroscope, which is the product of experience, values, and evolution, is hardly unerring, but it is far more effective than any train of logic. In *Personal Knowledge*, scientist-philosopher Michael Polanyi explained that relatively few lucky people have the ability to *think* their way through most situations. Instead they go through "the usual process of unconscious trial and error by which we *feel our way* to success and may continue to improve . . . without specifiably knowing how we do it."

Success hinges on people feeling free to act on their instincts. In *Blink*, Malcolm Gladwell tells the story of a fireman who ordered all his men out of a house before it collapsed. He was hard-pressed to explain why he thought collapse was imminent; later investigation revealed that what looked like a kitchen fire was in fact raging in the basement. The fireman subconsciously felt the heat coming from the floor.

For routine tasks, the conscious brain usually takes a back seat to instinct. Mike Rose, in *The Mind at Work*, observed how plumbers, waitresses, and others do their jobs. What he found was that they "disappear . . . into the task," reacting without conscious thought to the numerous subtle factors confronting them. The carpenter can tell by the sound of the saw that the cut will not be proper. The waitress can prioritize service on a busy day by reading the anxiety levels of different people. Judgment is reflected generally in action, not conscious thought: "our knowing is *in* our action."

In more complex tasks, the active brain still takes cues from instincts. In *Complications*, Dr. Atul Gawande writes about how surgeons feel their way through a bloody cavity to find and clamp the broken artery. "What you find when you get in close . . ." Gawande writes, "close enough to see the furrowed brows, the doubts and missteps, the failures as well as the successes, is how messy, uncertain, and also surprising medicine turns out to be. . . . The thing that still startles me is how fundamentally human an endeavor it is."

Inserting legal justification into daily choices injects this hidden process with a self-consciousness that, at least much of the time, is the path to failure. Polanyi describes how making someone self-conscious about what he knows how to do causes him to falter and often fail. A pianist can't play if he thinks about how he's hitting the notes. Professor Richard Arum, in his influential study on the effects of law on disorder in schools, *Judging School Discipline*, explains how legal systems disorient teachers: "[I]t is this hesitation, doubt, and weakening of conviction . . . that has undermined the effectiveness of school discipline."

Surely, you might say, people can explain why they did something. Indeed, but only to a point. An explanation can help the listener form his own judgment. Facts are always important. For tough choices, "sleeping on it" often allows our subconscious wisdom to seep into our conscious understanding. But these feelings and judgments rarely rise to the level of proof. Judgment is a black box. Psychologists Richard Nisbett and Timothy Wilson conducted a study that concluded that people have an innate *inability* to report accurately on their cognitive processes, typically coming up "with a plausible cause" instead of basing the explanation on "any true introspection." Police officers who catch a criminal often have a terrible time explaining why they felt there was "probable cause" to stop the criminal in the first place. So they make up reasons, part of a phenomenon known as "testi-lying."

To the modern mind, individual judgment is unsatisfactory as an organizing principle because judgment can vary widely. Reasonable people can approach the same problem very differently; this life truth is learned by every child watching her parents disagree. Human variability is a nightmare to legal planners looking for all decisions to be based on objective logic. But it is precisely this originality that gives freedom its power. Determined humans can accomplish amazing things if allowed to do it themselves. There are a thousand ways, as they say, to skin a cat.

The utopian aspiration of choices rolling off an assembly line of logic always results in a wreckage of the original goals. "It is a profoundly erroneous truism," philosopher and mathematician Alfred North Whitehead observed, "that we should cultivate the habit of thinking of what we are doing."

> The precise opposite is the case. Civilization advances by extending the number of important operations which we can perform without thinking about them. Operations of thought are like cavalry charges in a battle—they are strictly limited in number, they require fresh horses, and must only be made at decisive moments.

Tocqueville understood this perfectly: "If man were forced do demonstrate for himself all the truths of which he makes daily use, his task would never end. He would exhaust his strength in preparatory demonstration without ever advancing beyond them."

Freedom is not argument, or explanation, or plausible justifications. Freedom is mainly choice and action. To restore our freedom, we have to purge law from most daily activities. "Good and bad are but names very readily transferable to that or this," Emerson explained. "The only right is what is after my constitution, the only wrong what is against it. . . . We cannot spend the day in explanation."

The test of your judgment is not your justification but the judgment of others. Reclaiming the freedom to do whatever you want, or what feels right to you, requires one condition: Others have the same freedom, including the freedom to make judgments about you. The path back to freedom is letting all citizens, especially those in positions of leadership, be free to act on their best judgment.

LIBERATING LEADERSHIP

"When I was growing up," Joe Tanner remembers, "teaching was an honorable profession . . . My parents were both teachers, and they were held in high esteem in our community, like doctors and lawyers. They helped form the character of generations of young people." Public service was also honorable, and Tanner had a distinguished career in a variety of public jobs, including as head of Georgia's Department of Natural Resources. It was Tanner who, working with Governor Zell Miller, organized the overhaul of Georgia's public administration to release state employees from the bondage of civil service.

Most adults of a certain age remember a time when teachers were role models, not just people on the clock. Unimaginable as it may seem today, lawyers were the "aristocrats," Fareed Zakaria recalls, respected for their integrity. Doctors cared for the indigent as well as those who could pay. Political leaders were at the top of the social order. Society was hardly perfect, but there was a sense that people were important to each other. Standing in the community meant something. We were in it together.

How times have changed. The general sense today is that teachers are losers, lawyers are sleazy, doctors are greedy, and public service is the job of last resort. Politicians are hypocrites. Community is a hollow word. Money is what matters. There is almost no sense of responsibility for each other. This is not the profile of a healthy society.

Times are also different, of course—global forces and information technology have eroded community cohesion. But the main change is that people with responsibility no longer feel free to exercise personal leadership. Instead they slog through law all day. It was inevitable, over time, that this powerlessness would lead them to redirect their energies toward self-protection rather than accomplishment and reputation.

The opportunity to make a difference is as important now as it ever was. How teachers, doctors, religious leaders, and supervisors do their jobs affects everyone around them. The broader forces of our time also cry out for decisions. All these opportunities to make a difference lie before us, in plain sight, but made unreachable by an invisible wall of law. These choices used to be made by people we call leaders, a group that properly includes teachers and others who have responsibility on the ground, as well as judges, officials, and political figures. But they no longer feel free to grab hold of a problem and fix it.

Modern law strives to guarantee that decisions by leaders are correct. This hasn't worked, as we've seen. The flaw in the premise is that there is no correctness, at least not that can be proved. Choices are too complex. Judgment by leaders is even less susceptible to objective proof than other choices.

Truth lies not at the center of any matter, historian Henry Thomas Buckle suggested, but at the edges, where it intersects with all other matters. Too much safety means kids don't stay healthy. A preoccupation with one person's rights means other people get hurt. No decision can be judged from one point of view. All life is interconnected, in ways that we can only partially comprehend.

Choices by leaders involve uncertainties, trade-offs, risks, and balancing. The higher up the chain of responsibility, the greater the range of complexities and trade-offs. A tax dollar used for one purpose is not available to a thousand other worthy causes.

While most choices are too complex to dissect into objective parts, humans are nonetheless adept at making decisions. Life isn't this hard. Until our modern experiment with law everywhere, people just decided. Yes or no, then move on. When disputes occurred, someone up a hierarchy decided, saying something like "Sure, that seems sensible" or, "Oh, I wouldn't do it that way." That was it, or some expanded version of that. There was no legal argument, and no hearings, at least for choices outside the courtroom. The chain of accountability stretched upward until, in a democracy, it circled back to the vote of the people. A social structure of decisions up a hierarchy is not perfect, of course, but it's highly efficient.

Having a decision-maker is indispensable. That's how every enterprise works. A crowded society cannot operate without these choices by people in positions of leadership. "Wherever and whenever one person is found adequate to the discharge of a duty," George Washington noted, "it is worse executed by two persons, and scarcely done at all if three or more are employed." Just give people the responsibility, and see how they do.

Unavoidable nervousness surrounds all authority, but the risks of unfair results are far less than the risks of legal paralysis. Leadership is not arbitrary power. Leadership in most enterprises is a conditional responsibility, always subject to the judgment of someone else up the line. The nature of responsibility is that it puts people on the spot. That spotlight shines brighter the higher we go up the ladder. The more choices someone is able to make, the more checked he will be by public scrutiny. "There is no danger in power, if only it be not irresponsible," Woodrow Wilson said, but "if it be divided . . . it is obscured; and if it be obscured it is made irresponsible."

Leadership used to be the highest aspiration in American culture. We revere leaders in American history not because of their logic and capacity to argue, but because of their wisdom and character. Leaders are called upon to think for themselves, weighing the context and drawing on their inner forces of skill and values. "We may also say of Lincoln," Woodrow Wilson observed, "that he saw things always with his own eyes." An effective leader does not hew to the path of legal conformity, but will almost always make choices that are unexpected. "Effective leadership has to be based on intuitions that are correct," management expert Chester Barnard concluded, "notwithstanding doctrines that deny their correctness."

Probably the most important leadership trait is character—a concept that embodies faithfulness to doing what's right. Leaders of good character engender social trust, and thereby enable us to interact freely without fear. The litmus test of leadership is trust by others. "The only definition of a leader," Peter Drucker said, "is someone who has followers." Leaders earn this stature not by an unblemished record of success but by our evaluation of the whole person. Emerson, more than any other, focused on the trustworthiness of personal character. "The force of character," he observed, "is cumulative." Argument is just noise—a man who is respected "speak[s] from his character, and not from his tongue." George Washington is the archetype leader: "The heavy, leaden eyes turn on you, as the eyes of an ox in the pasture," Emerson wrote, "and the mouth has gravity and depth of quiet, as if this *man* had absorbed all the serenity of America, and left none for his restless . . . countrymen."

Legal accountability, by contrast, is a concept of argument. Anyone can complain, and often throw a monkey wrench into a perfectly good plan just by threatening a legal proceeding. Instead of aspiring to the common good, law drives decisions toward the lowest common denominator. It's closer to anarchy than hierarchy. Pretty soon people go through the day looking over their shoulders. Law leads to powerlessness. Character is irrelevant in a legalistic culture. We all know the drill: Focus on the rules; fill out the forms; answer to anyone who disagrees; prove it to me; prove it to them; that's just your point of view. We flail away in this legalistic morass, with no way to make sense of public choices and getting more tangled up every year.

We have to make a choice: It's either leaders or lawyers.

Stick with the lawyers, some say. America has exactly the system it wants. Philosophers such as Erich Fromm have argued that the legal cage we've built for ourselves just reflects our own "fear of freedom." Leszek Kolakowski suggests that we "expect from the state ever more solutions not only to social questions but also to private problems . . . that if we are not perfectly happy it's the state's fault." I don't ultimately agree with them, at least not for most people. These are symptoms of social failure, not causes. There are plenty of Americans who, if given the chance, will reach out to take responsibility. Americans hate this overlawyered system, surveys repeatedly show. The main reason it stays in place, in my view, is that we're still reeling from guilt, mainly over racism, and can't bear the thought of another unfair official. "The modern mind, tortured by moral self-doubt," Michael Polanyi observed, reaches for systemic solutions to "satisfy its passion for ruthless objectivity."

Leadership scares us. It's personal, and hinges on the character and wisdom of the particular person. Undoubtedly some percentage of judges, officials, and teachers will be incompetent or unfair. Accountability doesn't seem good enough—isn't there some system in which correctness can be guaranteed? Maybe we could go online and order up leaders of unimpeachable integrity. A reincarnation of George Washington would be perfect. Even better that he's not alive, so as not to inspire jealousies of wanting to switch places. A solemn voice, disembodied, gives us the answers. This miracle of a consensus leader is unlikely, however. So we sit on the fence, hating lawyers and scared of leaders.

Our hand-wringing about the fallibility of leaders misses the critical distinction between the two systems. The point is not that leaders will always be fairer than a legal proceeding. Fairness, as I've discussed, is always in the eye of the beholder. The important distinction is that leadership shifts the goal—from the individual to the common good. That's the job of a leader—to make choices for the common enterprise. Restoring a hierarchy of leadership dramatically alters the dynamic of public choices, with benefits that cascade through society and to our own freedoms. Here are a few of the virtues:

1. Leadership tends to promote compromise. Reasonableness matters, because the decision maker is trying to accommodate different points of view. Leaders have a gravitational pull toward the center—with effective leaders, all draw close to argue their point of view. Arguments over legal entitlements, by contrast, promote polarization. Lawyers tend to argue in extremes.

2. Leadership elevates the importance of ethical conduct and social sharing. People are judged in the round, not in legalistic snippets. As reputation becomes important again, social values turn outward, away from selfishness toward conduct that advances the common good.

3. Leaders can make the case for responsible decisions for a better tomorrow. Legalistic systems, by contrast, are dominated by short-term selfish demands. Fiscal responsibility requires leadership, not self-interested legal arguments.

4. Leaders empower the rest of us—our ideas matter only if someone with responsibility has the power to act on them. That's why strong principals are critical to teacher empowerment. We can make a difference only if there's a person with authority to implement our ideas.

5. Leadership is the hub of accountability. When something doesn't work out, leaders are accountable. Today there's no one to blame. The system's at fault. Look at the culture of government. Without leaders to make choices or to hold accountable, government is dead in the water.

Americans haven't seen much leadership recently, particularly from the political sector. That's one of the reasons we fear it. Americans have no muscle memory of the dynamics of compromise and character, at least not in public choices.

Reviving a culture of leadership requires not only legal authority, but an active delegation of responsibility as far down the chain as is practical. It's not surprising that Americans are reluctant to embrace leaders when law has removed their own authority to lead. Former Senator Bill Bradley has talked about how "looking to only two sources of solutions—government or market—is like sitting on a two-legged stool. The third leg of the stool—civil society—is missing." Civil society is missing because it was suffocated by centralized bureaucracy. Just as we must clean out Washington, we must also restore the conditions for people to make a difference.

Radical decentralization is needed to inspire interest and trust in public choices. A "centralized administration is fit only to enervate," Tocqueville noted. That's why he believed local government is the cornerstone of our democracy: "Municipal institutions constitute the strength of free nations. Town meetings are to liberty what primary schools are to science; they bring it within the people's reach, they teach men how to use and how to enjoy it . . . without municipal institutions it cannot have the spirit of liberty."

Centralization, whether by overbearing law or by tyranny, suffocates the human spirit and, with it, the public spirit as well. This is why Rome grew weak and fell, as historian Hugh Trevor-Roper describes in his introduction to *The Decline and Fall of the Roman Empire*: "The centralization, the immobility, the monopoly of the Roman Empire had gradually destroyed that pluralism, stifled those ideas, and progress had been retarded, public virtues had declined, and in the end an inert, top-heavy political structure had fallen to external blows which a healthier organism would have survived."

Only by taking responsibility themselves will Americans become strong citizens, comfortable again with the trade-offs and other benefits of leadership at higher levels of responsibility. Schools are an obvious place to begin using these muscles. Social services can also be decentralized—drawing on the goodwill and energy in local charities and faith-based organizations. A mandatory national service can educate the leaders of tomorrow in the nuances of social choices and the discipline of making judgments for the future. Havel states the need plainly:

> A modern democratic state cannot consist merely of civil service, political parties and private enterprises. It must offer citizens a colorful array of ways to become involved, both privately and publicly. . . . In a richly layered civil society, a vital . . . role is played not only by the organs of administration, but also by . . . a broad array of civic associations, groups and clubs. All of this together is what creates the life-giving environment for politics.

Reviving the freedom to make a difference requires a new legal structure that leaves room for local initiative and authority. Delegation downward, known as "subsidiarity" in Catholic doctrine, is a core tenet of practical management: "Control what you must, not what you can." The positive effects will not be hard to discern. Wherever local leadership is allowed, the community will be transformed. The goals will change—from selfishness to a sense of common ownership. Local responsibility will unleash individual resourcefulness. The culture will blossom, as it does at TEAM Academy. What Americans will come to see, when law is pulled away from daily choices and replaced by people with responsibility, is that public choices will become moderate rather than extreme, with most people striving for balance rather than victory.

Bringing public choices into the realm of real people was, of course, one of the founding ideas of our Republic. It was the source of the social strength that Tocqueville referred to as "self-interest, rightly understood." Decentralizing local services has a cost, of course: Things won't be standardized. Havel sees this as a virtue:

"Life is . . . nonstandard." People can still be accountable up the chain of authority for their conduct and results. They're just not told how to do things. They reach inside themselves to make sense of daily challenges.

I can already hear the chorus of the status quo. Who's to say what good values are? Look at our history of racism and other bad values. That's why, they say, we have no choice but to build law into daily transactions. But the cure to bad values, as noted earlier, is to demand good values. Running authority through a legal gauntlet just discourages people in authority from asserting any values. We end up getting the values of whoever pounds the table for himself.

But Americans don't share values anymore, the chorus retorts. Indeed, humans will inevitably apply their own values to each situation. But the inevitability of disagreement is precisely why we need leaders to make choices. It's also unclear how much Americans disagree on basic issues—say, the need to maintain classroom order or to keep lawsuits within reasonable bounds. Sociologist Alan Wolfe and others have found broad agreement on important social values.

If people share these values, the chorus shouts back, why don't they act on them? Here we get to the source of all this mischief. Those virtues have eroded not because Americans changed their minds, but because American law stopped protecting good values. When leadership was put on ice, self-interested people learned they could argue almost anything. Some started pushing the envelope. This set in motion a downward spiral of selfishness and fear. Values frayed because no one took the authority to defend them.

Without room for leadership it is almost impossible for a culture to maintain a moral compass. America was not built by our constitutional structure. It was built by real people who asserted their values within a legal structure designed to promote those free choices. The morality of our culture resides in individuals—not in law or any other institutional systems. Institutions are fundamentally less capable of moral acts, as Niebuhr observed, because individuals don't feel personally responsible: "[T]here is less reason to guide and to check impulse, less capacity for self-transcendence, less ability to comprehend the needs of others." Like all institutions, law takes a life of its own, developing a kind of "rule narcissism" in which people don't even think about right and wrong. Only when we restore responsibility to individuals—real people charged with deciding right and wrong—can America reclaim a coherent public morality.

Since the beginning of the Industrial Revolution, America has addressed the conflicts in an interdependent society by enacting ever more law. Now we're bogged down in all this law, without personal freedom or the ability to accomplish our public goals. We must return to first principles and confront the challenges of modernism by using the powers of freedom, not by removing them. The vision of a society in which people can make a difference is not hard to conceive—where teachers take back control of classrooms, judges draw boundaries, and the rest of us are invested in these and other public choices.

Restoring the conditions for leadership will itself require extraordinary leadership. No invitation will arrive from Washington asking us to fix this mess. "Once 'active virtue' is lost in a society," historian Hugh Trevor-Roper observed when discussing the decline of Rome, "it is hard to recover, perhaps impossible without radical social change; and the survival of nations may sometimes depend on the life of one man." We must grab hold of this problem ourselves.

There's no need, as mentioned earlier, to have official power—officials are immobilized anyway. The task is to galvanize the will of the people behind a shift in authority structures toward personal responsibility and accountability. Trust in leadership is the hard part, and this quiet revolution must be championed by people who do not themselves aspire to official position. Their credibility will shine brighter because they aspire to a better society, not to higher office.

In his departing speech as general, George Washington described the new nation, which, he believed, would enable people to be "actors in a most conspicuous theatre . . . designed . . . for the display of human greatness and felicity." Freedom is supposed to be about originality and spontaneity, not a stultifying system of rules and justification. In the American brand of freedom, people can invent themselves, and follow their instincts and passions, make guesses and be lucky, and get past bad luck with determination. Human energy explodes all over the place. People agree and disagree, and then move on. It's the best system ever invented. American history proves it. All this energy and imagination can be applied to remake our social structure.

There's no rule that says we can't change the rules. America is ours for the taking. People without immediate self-interest must come together, as our founders did, and assert our authority as citizens to bring common sense back to America. Lawyers quibble. Leaders make things happen.

LOOKING AT AMERICA FROM A DISTANCE

Anthropologist Jared Diamond in *Collapse* shows how bad habits can, over time, destroy a culture. Many societies that fail take some important resource for granted and deplete it without understanding the long-term consequences—for example, cutting down all the trees on Easter Island or the early Nordic settlers in Greenland allowing sheep to graze on grass that wouldn't grow back.

America's greatest natural resource is a culture that unleashed the power of individuals. Other countries, including nations with advanced educational systems and vast natural resources, do not share this sense of individual initiative. But that spirit of the free individual erodes if we don't let people exercise it. Listen to the people who teach in our schools. Look at the decline of civic involvement. Watch the health care system, like a flower in its last full bloom, as it provides miracle cures while millions are uninsured and thousands die of infections contracted in hospitals.

When civilizations start to fail, Diamond found, they often refuse to adapt. In Greenland the population starved to death rather than adapt to dietary habits of the native Inuit, eating fish and seals. Cultural values, Diamond discovered, are often stronger than good sense. The new American ideology of controlling decisions by other people, forged in the cultural cauldron of the 1960s, has become a similarly powerful habit.

Distrust has overpowered our good sense. We know in our hearts that teachers need the authority to run a classroom, and that judges should be able to dismiss frivolous and extreme lawsuits. But the possibility of an unfair teacher, or an unfair judge, seems too much for us to contemplate. We want every human encounter to be perfect. This is crazy, of course. "The pursuit of ever more perfect accountability," philosopher Onora O'Neill observes, "builds a culture of suspicion. . . . Plants don't flourish when we pull them up too often to check how their roots are growing."

But distrust is hard to fight. All someone needs to do is paint some nightmare scenario, and people flee back into the maw of law. Distrust also has an addictive quality. There's no small amount of pleasure in disdain and contempt. Philosopher William Hazlitt once wrote an essay entitled "On the Pleasure of Hating," in which he said that "hating, like a poisonous mineral, eats into the heart." Wallowing in distrust is one of the sick pleasures of Washington— political junkies get together to outdo each other. Visit the Web sites of the religious right: "Liberals are evil, anti-American [and] unpatriotic, . . . trying their best to extinguish our nation." Or the liberal left: "The Republican party is a criminal conspiracy to betray the interests of the American people in favor of . . . corporate interests and absolutist religious groups."

Like most addictions, this compulsion for distrust is self-destructive. In *The Moral Basis of a Backward Society*, sociologist Edward Banfield describes how cultural norms of distrust caused a small town in southern Italy in the 1950s to be mired in poverty and ignorance. "The inability of villagers to act together for their common good," Banfield found, was grounded in an assumption that people would act only for their "immediate, material interest." Neighbors were unable to pool small plots of land for more efficient farming because of an assumption that the other people wouldn't pull their weight. Having given up on getting ahead, people focused on making sure others didn't get ahead either. One farmer who planted six fruit trees woke up to find them cut down. Fathers taught their sons never to tell the truth of what they owned—because that would be an invitation to theft or vandalism. Villagers dealt with others only with "the greatest suspicion." The mayor of a village turned down a gift of money from Americans to help needy children because, he said sadly, the citizens would "soon ask . . . how much I had kept for myself." In this culture of distrust, there were "no leaders and no followers."

Banfield's village descended much further into the pit of distrust than America has. But the trend is the same. In America as well, people are pursuing a goal of "immediate material interest" instead of cooperation in social dealings. Our obsessive distrust of judges and anyone else with authority is not that different from the villagers' distrust of the mayor, causing him to turn down a gift to the town. The partisan efforts to polarize American society—say, debates over gay marriage or flag burning—are not far removed from the destructive acts of a jealous neighbor in Banfield's village.

Trust is an essential element of a free society, as Nobel laureate Kenneth Arrow explained, because it allows people to focus on moving forward toward their goals rather than looking over their shoulders. This trust is not blind faith in any particular person—we all carry a little caution when dealing with others—but trust in the values of society and its governing institutions. I don't suspect a mass movement will form under the banner "Let's Trust Government" or "Power to the Judges." What's called for is not to give officials carte blanche, but to exercise our collective will to delegate responsibility to make common choices. The freedom of leaders to make these choices comes with exposure to judgments by others up the chain of responsibility, and eventually back to the ballot box. Everyone is accountable. You can help see to it. You're free too. Free choice, not legal bickering, is how a free society thrives.

History tells us that social change occurs only in times of crisis. Among other reasons, that's when people, out of desperation, are willing to become followers. Failure alone is not sufficient. "The more miserable a man is, the more he dreads every sort of change," Kropotkin observed, "lest it may make him more wretched still." Machiavelli believed that the intensity of special interests usually trumps the general will of the public—mainly because the public is cynical about the capacity to reform anything. Only extraordinary leaders can lead a society out of this spiral of distrust, Machiavelli believed—people who somehow inspire the public confidence by their character and vision.

There's a countertrend working in our favor—a cycle of social change in America, as I note in the introduction, that seems to occur every thirty years or so. The last was in the 1960s, so we're past due. The mood is for change; Americans are fed up with overbearing laws and legal threats. The needed changes do not, by and large, require a shift in moral values—the challenge is to rebuild authority structures to implement our values. The growing burden of health care costs and failing schools may finally precipitate reform. Or maybe it will be the idiocies of child-raising: not letting children wander out to play, and handcuffing them when they misbehave in school. I don't know what will provide the spark. But I think I know what's missing.

To confront the challenges of our time, Americans must be free to take responsibility. This in turn requires a legal revolution, clearing out decades of accumulated law and bureaucracy—and building instead a legal framework that defines and protects an open field of human freedom. This project, of historic dimension, is worth the effort. It is how we take control of our future. It is how we become confident again. Liberating America's can-do spirit will work miracles.

AGENDA FOR CHANGE
AND
REFERENCES

AGENDA FOR CHANGE

The proposals in this book are based on core principles concerning the structure of freedom, principles that have been largely forgotten in the expansion of modern law. Working together, Americans can build support for fundamental changes needed to restore our freedom to make sensible daily choices, along the following lines:

PRINCIPLES FOR DAILY FREEDOM

1. Restore the authority of judges to draw legal boundaries so that people have confidence that justice will be reliable.
2. Replace the vocabulary of rights with the goal of balance.
3. Liberate teachers and principals from legal rules and processes. Bureaucracy can't teach.
4. Restore responsibility to government by giving authority to identifiable officials.
5. Provide checks and balances for official decisions up the hierarchy of responsibility, not generally by legal proceedings by dissatisfied individuals. The goal is the common good, not the lowest common denominator.

6. Revive personal accountability. Your freedom hinges on the freedom of others to make judgments about you.
7. Decentralize public services to the extent feasible. Citizenship requires active involvement in the community.
8. Organize a national civic leadership to propose a radical overhaul of government. Washington is paralyzed and must be recodified. This requires outside leadership.

GETTING INVOLVED

If you would like to help liberate teachers, doctors, or yourselves from the quagmire of too much law, or have questions or ideas, here are three resources and organizations in which I am actively involved and that can refer you to other resources in specific areas:

Common Good. Common Good is building coalitions of national and local organizations behind a fundamental overhaul of American law and government, including planning pilot projects for expert health courts, devising new protocols for discipline in schools, drawing up new standards for children's play, and working with leading judges and legal scholars to restore the authority of judges to draw the boundaries of unreasonable claims and defenses. Common Good is nonpartisan and has attracted the support of prominent citizens from both the right and the left, from consumer advocates as well as leaders of business and nonprofits. For information, visit Common Good at www.commongood.org.

NewTalk.org. A group of nonprofit organizations led by Common Good is hosting online forums of thought leaders at newtalk. org. These discussions encompass a wide range of public policy topics, focusing on topics that the political system has difficulty being honest about. NewTalk invites comments from readers, including suggestions for future topics and participants.

Lifewithoutlawyers.com. I will be collecting reactions and ideas for change and responding to questions on this Web site. Please let me know what you think. The Web site will also have a schedule of events and activities related to this book.

REFERENCES

NOTES

The Notes can be found at www.lifewithoutlawyers.com.

BIBLIOGRAPHY

Almond, Gabriel, and Sidney Verba, eds. *The Civic Culture Revisited*. London: Sage Publications, 1980.

Alschuler, Alfred, ed. *Teacher Burnout*. Washington, DC: National Education Association, 1980.

Amar, Akhil Reed, and Alan R. Hirsch. *For the People: What the Constitution Really Says about Your Rights*. New York: Touchstone, 1999.

Anechiarico, Frank, and James B. Jacobs. *The Pursuit of Absolute Integrity: How Corruption Control Makes Government Ineffective*. Chicago: University of Chicago Press, 1996.

Arendt, Hannah. *The Portable Hannah Arendt*. Edited by Peter Baehr. New York: Penguin, 2000.

Arendt, Hannah. *Between Past and Future*. New York: Penguin, 1968.

Arum, Richard. *Judging School Discipline: The Crisis of Moral Authority*. Cambridge, MA: Harvard University Press, 2005.

Atiyah, P. S. "From Principle to Pragmatism," 65 *Iowa Law Review* 1249 (1980).

Atkinson, Terry, and Guy Claxton. *The Intuitive Practitioner: On the Value of Not Always Knowing What One Is Doing*. Buckingham, UK: Open University Press, 2000.

Bai, Matt. *The Argument: Billionaires, Bloggers, and The Battle to Remake Democratic Politics*. New York: Penguin, 2007.

Bailyn, Bernard, ed. *The Debate on the Constitution*. New York: Library of America, 1993.

Banfield, Edward. *The Moral Basis of a Backward Society*. New York: Free Press, 1958.

Barak, Aharon. *Judicial Discretion*. New Haven, CT: Yale University Press, 1989.

Barber, Benjamin. *Strong Democracy: Participatory Politics for a New Age*. Berkeley: University of California Press, 2004.

Barnard, Chester. *The Functions of the Executive*. Cambridge, MA: Harvard University Press, 1966.

Barzun, Jacques. *Of Human Freedom*. Philadelphia: J. P. Lippincott Company, 1939.

Barzun, Jacques. *From Dawn to Decadence: 500 Years of Western Cultural Life; 1500 to the Present*. New York: HarperCollins, 2000.

Barzun, Jacques. *A Stroll with William James*. Chicago: University of Chicago Press, 2002.

Baumol, William J., Robert E. Litan, and Carl J. Schramm. *Good Capitalism, Bad Capitalism, and the Economics of Growth and Prosperity*. New Haven, CT: Yale University Press, 2007.

Beard, Charles A., and Mary R. Beard. *The Rise of American Civilization*. New York: MacMillian, 1930.

Beckman, Lisa F., and Ichiro Kawachi, eds. *Social Epidemiology*. Oxford: Oxford University Press, 2000.

Bellah, Robert N., Richard Madsen, William M. Sullivan, Ann Swidler, and Steven M. Tipton. *The Good Society*. New York: Vintage, 1991.

Bellah, Robert N., Richard Madsen, William M. Sullivan, Ann Swidler, and Steven M. Tipton. *Habits of the Heart: Individualism and Commitment in American Life*. Berkeley: University of California Press, 1996.

Bennis, Warren G. *Why Leaders Can't Lead: The Unconscious Conspiracy Continues*. San Francisco: Jossey-Bass, 1989.

Berlin, Isaiah. *The Proper Study of Mankind: An Anthology of Essays*. Edited by Henry Hardy and Roger Hausheer. New York: Farrar, Straus and Giroux, 2000.

Berlin, Isaiah. *Four Essays on Liberty*. Oxford: Oxford University Press, 1992.

Berlin, Isaiah. *The Crooked Timber of Humanity*. New York: Knopf, 1991.

Bestor, Arthur. *Educational Wastelands: The Retreat from Learning in Our Public Schools*. Champaign, IL: University of Illinois Press, 1985.

Black, Donald J. "The Mobilization of Law," 2 *J. Legal Studies* 125, 131 n. 24 (1973).

Bok, Edward. *The Americanization of Edward Bok: The Autobiography of a Dutch Boy Fifty Years After*. New York: Cosimo, 2005.

Boorstin, Daniel J. *The Americans: The Democratic Experience*. New York: Vintage, 1974.

Bovens, Mark. *Quest for Responsibility: Accountability and Citizenship in Complex Organizations*. Cambridge: Cambridge University Press, 1998.

Bozeman, Barry. Bureaucracy and Red Tape. Upper Saddle River, NJ: Prentice-Hall, 2000.

Bradley, Bill. *The New American Story*. New York: Random House, 2008.

Breyer, Stephen G. *Breaking the Vicious Circle*. Cambridge, MA: Harvard University Press, 1993.

Brooks, Robert, and Sam Goldstein. *Raising Resilient Children: Fostering Strength, Hope and Optimism in Your Child*. Chicago: Contemporary Books, 2001.

Brownlee, Shannon. *Overtreated: Why Too Much Medicine Is Making Us Sicker and Poorer*. New York: Bloomsbury, 2007.

Calabresi, Guido, and Philip Bobbitt. *Tragic Choices*. New York: W. W. Norton, 1978.

Caldwell, Lynton K. *The Administrative Theories of Hamilton and Jefferson: Their Contribution to Thought on Public Administration*. New York: Russell & Russell, 1964.

Callahan, David. *The Cheating Culture*. New York: Harcourt, 2004.

Cardozo, Benjamin N. *The Nature of the Judicial Process*. Buffalo, NY: Hein, 1997.

Cardozo, Benjamin N. *The Growth of the Law*. New Haven, CT: Yale University Press, 1924.

Chubb, John E., and Terry M. Moe. *Politics, Markets, and America's Schools*. Washington, DC: Brookings Institution, 1990.

Cohen, Eliot A. *Booknotes: On American Character*. Edited by Brian Lamb. New York: Public Affairs, 2005.

Commager, Henry Steele. *The American Mind*. New Haven, CT: Yale University Press, 1959.

Cook, Karen, ed. *Trust in Society*. New York: Russell Sage Foundation, 2001.

Damasio, Antonio. *Descartes' Error*. New York: Avon Books, 1994.

Damon, William. *The Path to Purpose: Helping Our Children Find Their Calling in Life*. New York: Free Press, 2008.

Damon, William, Howard Gardner, and Mihaly Csikszentmihalyi. *Good Work*. New York: Basic Books, 2001.

De Tocqueville, Alexis. *Democracy in America*. Translated by Henry Reeve and Francis Bowen, edited by Phillips Bradley. 2 vols. New York: Vintage, 1990.

Diamond, Jared. *Collapse: How Societies Choose to Fail or Succeed*. New York: Penguin, 2005.

Dickens, Charles. *American Notes*. New York: Modern Library, 1996.

Douglas, Mary, and Aaron Wildavsky. *Risk and Culture*. Berkeley: University of California Press, 1982.

Dreyfus, Hubert L., and Stuart E. Dreyfus. *Mind Over Machine: The Power of Human Intuition and Expertise in the Era of the Computer*. New York: Free Press, 1986.

Drucker, Peter F. *The Essential Drucker: The Best of Sixty Years of Peter Drucker's Essential Writings on Management*. New York: HarperCollins, 2003.

Drucker, Peter F. *The Age of Discontinuity*. New Brunswick, NJ: Transaction Books, 1992.

Drucker, Peter F. *Concept of the Corporation*. New York: Mentor, 1964.

Durkheim, Emile. *Moral Education*. Translated by Everett K. Wilson and Herman Schnurer. Mineola, NY: Courier Dover, 2002.

Durkheim, Emile. *Emile Durkheim: Selected Writings*. Edited and translated by Anthony Giddens. Cambridge, UK: Cambridge University Press, 1972.

Dworkin, Ronald. *Taking Rights Seriously*. Cambridge, MA: Harvard University Press, 2007.

Edwards, John. *Four Trials*. New York: Simon & Schuster, 2004.

Ellickson, Robert C. *Order without Law: How Neighbors Settle Disputes*. Cambridge, MA: Harvard University Press, 1991.

Ely, John Hart. *Democracy and Distrust: A Theory of Judicial Review*. Cambridge, MA: Harvard University Press, 1980.

Emerson, Ralph Waldo. *Essays and Lectures*. New York: Library of America, 1983.

Emerson, Ralph Waldo. *Journals of Ralph Waldo Emerson*. New York: Houghton Mifflin, 1912.

Evans, Harold, Gail Buckland, and David Lefer. *They Made America: From the Steam Engine to the Search Engine; Two Centuries of Innovators*. New York: Little, Brown, 2004.

Etzioni, Amitai. *The New Golden Rule*. New York: Basic Books, 1996.

Etzioni, Amitai. *Rights and the Common Good*. New York: St. Martin's, 1995.

Farber, Barry, ed. *Stress and Burnout in the Human Service Professions*. Oxford: Pergamon, 1983.

Fauconnier, Gilles, and Turner, Mark. *The Way We Think: Conceptual Blending and the Mind's Hidden Complexities*. New York: Basic Books, 2002.

Feeley, Malcolm M. *The Process Is the Punishment: Handling Cases in a Lower Criminal Court*. New York: Russell Sage Foundation, 1992.

Fish, Stanley. *The Trouble with Principle*. Cambridge, MA: Harvard University Press, 1999.

Fish, Stanley. "Dennis Martinez and the Uses of Theory," *Yale Law Journal*, vol. 96, no. 8 (July 1987), pp. 1773–1800.

Fisher, Sydney George. *The Struggle for American Independence*. Philadelphia: J. B. Lippincott Company, 1908.

Foner, Eric. *The Story of American Freedom*. New York: W. W. Norton, 1998.

Foster, Richard, and Sarah Kaplan. *Creative Destruction: Why Companies That Are Built to Last Underperform the Market—and How to Successfully Transform Them*. New York: Currency, 2001.

Foucault, Michel. *Discipline & Punish*. London: Penguin,1975.

Freedman, Miriam Kurztig. *School Law: Grades, Report Cards etc. . . . and the Law*. School Law Pro, 2005.

Fromm, Erich. *Escape from Freedom*. New York: Henry Holt, 1969.

Frost, Joe L., Pei-San Brown, John A. Sutterby, and Candra D. Thornton. *The Developmental Benefits of Playgrounds*. Olney, MD: Association for Childhood Education International, 2004.

Fukuyama, Francis. *Trust*. New York: Free Press, 1995.

Furedi, Frank. *Culture of Fear: Risk-taking and the Morality of Low Expectations*. London: Continuum, 2006.

Furedi, Frank. *Politics of Fear*. London: Continuum, 2007.

Garson, Barbara. *All the Livelong Day: The Meaning and Demeaning of Routine Work*. New York: Doubleday, 1972.

Gawande, Atul. *Complications: A Surgeon's Notes on an Imperfect Science*. New York: Macmillan, 2002.

Gawande, Atul. *Better: A Surgeon's Notes on Performance.* New York: Henry Holt, 2007.

Gaylin, Willard, and Bruce Jennings. *The Perversion of Autonomy: Coercion and Constraints in a Liberal Society.* Washington, DC: Georgetown University Press, 2003.

Gibbon, Edward. *The Decline and Fall of the Roman Empire.* Introduction by Hugh Trevor-Roper. 6 vols. New York: Everyman's Library, 1993.

Gill, Tim. *No Fear: Growing up in a Risk Averse Society.* London: Calouste, Gulbenkian, 2007.

Ginsburg, Kenneth R., et al. "The Importance of Play in Promoting Healthy Child Development and Maintaining Strong Parent-Child Bonds." American Academy of Pediatrics. 9 October 2006. http://www.aap.org/pressroom/play FINAL.pdf.

Gladwell, Malcom. *Blink: The Power of Thinking Without Thinking.* New York: Little, Brown, 2005.

Glendon, Mary Ann. *Rights Talk: The Impoverishment of Political Discourse.* New York: Free Press, 1991.

Goleman, Daniel. *Working with Emotional Intelligence.* New York: Bantam Books, 1998.

Gore, Al. *Common Sense Government.* Introduction by Philip K. Howard. New York: Random House, 1995.

Gore, Al. *Creating a Government that Works Better and Costs Less: The Report of the National Performance Review.* New York: Plume, 1993.

Gore, Al. *An Inconvenient Truth: The Planetary Emergency of Global Warming and What We Can Do about It.* New York: Rodale, 2006.

Grant, Gerald. *The World We Created at Hamilton High.* Cambridge, MA: Harvard University Press, 1988.

Graves, Donald. *The Energy to Teach.* Portsmouth, NH: Heinemann, 2001.

Green, David G. *We're (Nearly) All Victims Now!: How Political Correctness Is Undermining Our Liberal Culture.* London: Civitas, 2006.

Habermas, Jurgen. *The Inclusion of the Other: Studies in Political Theory.* Edited by Ciaran Cronin and Pablo De Greiff. Cambridge, MA: MIT Press, 2001.

Hahn, Robert W., ed. *Risks, Costs, and Lives Saved: Getting Better Results from Regulation.* Oxford: Oxford University Press, 1996.

Hammond, Kenneth R. *Human Judgment and Social Policy.* Oxford: Oxford University Press, 1996.

Harrison, Lawrence E., and Samuel P. Huntington. *Culture Matters: How Values Shape Human Progress.* New York: Basic Books, 2000.

Hart, H.L.A. *The Concept of Law.* London: Oxford University Press, 1961.

Hart, H.L.A. "Positivism and the Separation of Law and Morals," *Harvard Law Review,* 71 (1958): 623–624.

Havel, Vàclav. "The End of the Modern Era," *New York Times,* March 1, 1992.

Havel, Vàclav. *The Art of the Impossible: Politics and Morality in Practice.* New York: Knopf, 1997.

Hayek, Friedrich August. *The Constitution of Liberty*. Chicago: University of Chicago Press, 1978.

Hayek, Friedrich August. *Law, Legislation and Liberty*. Chicago: University Chicago Press, 1981.

Hazlitt, William. "On the Pleasure of Hating," *The Plain Speaker: The Key Essays*. Edited by Duncan Wu. Oxford: Blackwell, 1998.

Head, Simon. *The New Ruthless Economy*. New York: Oxford, 2003.

Heineman, Robert. *Authority and the Liberal Tradition*. New Brunswick, NJ: Transaction Books, 1994.

Himmelfarb, Gertrude. *The De-moralization of Society: From Victorian Virtues to Modern Values*. New York: Vintage, 1996.

Hobbes, Thomas. *Leviathan*. Edited by Richard E. Flathman and David Johnston. New York: W. W. Norton, 1996.

Hofstadter, Richard. *The American Political Tradition and the Men Who Made It*. New York: Vintage, 1955.

Hofstadter, Richard. *Anti-Intellectualism in American Life*. New York: Vintage, 1963.

Holmes, Oliver Wendell. *The Common Law*. Clark, NJ: The Lawbook Exchange, 2005.

Honig, Bonnie. *Democracy and the Foreigner*. Princeton, NJ: Princeton University Press, 2001.

Howard, Philip K. *The Death of Common Sense*. New York: Random House, 1995.

Howard, Philip K. *The Collapse of the Common Good*. New York: Ballantine, 2002.

Hsiao, Kung-Chuan. *A History of Chinese Political Thought*. Princeton, NJ: Princeton University Press, 1979.

Huber, Peter W. *Liability*. New York: Basic Books, 1998.

Huber, Peter W., and Robert E. Litan. *The Liability Maze: The Impact of Liability Law on Safety and Innovation*. Washington, DC: Brookings Institution, 1991.

Huber, Peter W. *Galileo's Revenge: Junk Science in the Courtroom*. New York: Basic Books, 1993.

Huizinga, Johan. *Homo Ludens: A Study of the Play Element in Culture*. Boston: Beacon, 1955.

Hummel, Ralph P. *The Bureaucratic Experience: A Critique of Life in the Modern Organization*. New York: St. Martin's Press, 1994.

Hunter, Gordon, ed. *Immigrant Voices: Twenty-four Narratives on Becoming an American*. New York: Signet, 1999.

Hunter, James Davison. *The Death of Character*. New York: Basic Books, 2000.

Huxley, Aldous. *Collected Essays by Aldous Huxley*. New York: Harper & Row Publishers, 1958.

Ingersoll, Richard M. *Who Controls Teachers' Work?: Power and Accountability in America's Schools*. Cambridge, MA: Harvard University Press, 2003.

Jackson, Philip W., Robert E. Boostrom, and David T. Hansen. *The Moral Life of Schools*. San Francisco: Jossey-Bass, 1993.

James, William. *Writings, 1878–1899*. Edited by Gerald E. Myers. New York: Library of America, 1992.

James, William. *Pragmatism and Other Writings*. New York: Penguin, 2000.

Jarvie, Ian Charles, and Sandra Pralong, eds. *Popper's Open Society after 50 Years*. London: Routledge, 1999.

Jefferson, Thomas. *Political Writings*. Edited by Joyce Appleby and Terence Ball. Cambridge: Cambridge University Press, 1999.

Jewkes, John, David Sawers, and Richard Stillerman. *The Sources of Invention*. New York: W. W. Norton, 1958.

Justinian. *Justinian's Institutes*. Translated by Peter Birks and Grant McLeod, edited by Paul Krueger. Ithaca, NY: Cornell University Press, 1987.

Kagan, Robert. *Adversarial Legalism: The American Way of Law*. Cambridge, NY: Harvard University Press, 2001.

Kaplow, Louis, and Steven Shavell. *Fairness Versus Welfare*. Cambridge, MA: Harvard University Press, 2002.

Karasek, Robert, and Tores Theorell. *Healthy Work*. New York: Basic Books, 1990.

Katzmann, Robert, ed. *The Law Firm and the Public Good*. Washington, DC: Brookings Institution, 1995.

Kaufman, Herbert. *Red Tape: Its Origins, Uses, and Abuses*. Washington, DC: Brookings Institution, 1977.

Kelman, Steven. *Procurement and Public Management: The Fear of Discretion and the Quality of Government Performance*. Washington, DC: The American Enterprise Institute Press, 1990.

Kennedy, Eugene, and Sara C. Charles. *Authority: The Most Misunderstood Idea in America*. New York: Free Press, 1997.

Kindon, Don. *Too Much of a Good Thing: Raising Children of Character in an Indulgent Age*. New York: Hyperion, 2001.

Klein, Gary. *Intuition at Work: Why Developing Your Gut Instinct Will Make You Better at What You Do*. New York: Doubleday, 2003.

Kolakowski, Leszek. *Modernity on Endless Trial*. Chicago: University of Chicago Press, 1990.

Kronman, Anthony. *The Lost Lawyer: Failing Ideas of the Legal Profession*. Cambridge, MA: Harvard University Press, 1993.

Kropotkin, Peter Alekseevich. *Anarchism: A Collection of Revolutionary Writings*. Edited by Roger N. Baldwin. Mineola, NY: Dover, 2002.

Kruger, Danny. *On Fraternity: Politics Beyond Liberty and Equality*. London: Civitas, 2007.

Lasch, Christopher. *The Revolt of the Elites and the Betrayal of Democracy*. New York: W. W. Norton, 1996.

Lasch, Christopher. *The Culture of Narcissism: American Life in an Age of Diminishing Expectations*. New York: W. W. Norton, 1979.

Lasch, Christopher. *The True and Only Heaven*. New York: W. W. Norton, 1991.

Leiter, Brian, ed. *Objectivity in Law and Morals*. Cambridge, UK: Cambridge University Press, 2001.

Light, Paul C. *Thickening Government: Federal Hierarchy and the Diffusion of Accountability*. Washington, DC: Brookings Institution, 1995.

Lightfoot, Sara Lawrence. *The Good High School: Portraits of Character and Culture*. New York: Basic Books, 1983.

Lincoln, Abraham. *Abraham Lincoln: Complete Works*. New York: The Century Co., 1907.

Lipsky, Michael. *Street Level Bureaucracy: Dilemmas of the Individual in Public Services*. New York: Russell Sage Foundation, 1980.

Locke, John. *Two Treatises of Government*. Montana: Kessinger, 2004.

Louv, Richard. *Last Child in the Woods: Saving Our Children from Nature-deficit Disorder*. Chapel Hill, SC: Algonquin Books of Chapel Hill, 2006.

Lowi, Theodore. *The End of Liberalism: The Second Republic of the United States*. New York: W. W. Norton, 1979.

Luhmann, Niklas. *Risk: A Sociological Theory*. New York: Aldine de Gruyter, 1993.

Machiavelli. *The Prince*. Edited by Albert Russell Ascoli, translated by Peter Constantine. New York: Modern Library, 2008.

Madison, James, Edward J. Larson, and Michael P. Winship. *The Constitutional Convention: A Narrative History from the Notes of James Madison*. New York: Modern Library, 2005.

Mann, Thomas E., and Norman J. Ornstein. *The Broken Branch: How Congress Is Failing America and How to Get It Back on Track*. Oxford: Oxford University Press, 2006.

Marano, Hara Estroff. *A Nation of Wimps: The High Cost of Invasive Parenting*. New York: Broadway, 2008.

McGregor, Douglas. *Human Side of Enterprise*. New York: McGraw-Hill, 1960.

McLynn, Frank. *Napoleon: A Biography*. New York: Arcade, 2002.

Melville, Herman. "Bartleby the Scrivener." In *Billy Budd and Other Tales*. New York: Penguin, 1986.

Menand, Louis. *The Metaphysical Club*. New York: Farrar, Straus and Giroux, 2001.

Mencken, H. L. *Mencken's America*. Athens, OH: Ohio University Press, 2004.

Mill, John Stuart. *On Liberty*. New York: Penguin, 1982.

Mill, John Stuart. *Principles of Political Economy*. New York: Penguin, 1985.

Miller, Matthew. *The 2% Solution: Fixing America's Problems in Ways Liberals and Conservatives Can Love*. New York: Public Affairs/Perseus, 2003.

Miller, Zell. *Listen to This Voice*. Macon, GA: Mercer University Press, 1998.

Morreim, E. Haavi. *Holding Health Care Accountable: Law and the New Medical Marketplace*. Oxford: Oxford University Press, 2001.

Moyers, Bill. *A World of Ideas*. New York: Doubleday, 1987.

Moynihan, Daniel Patrick. *Maximum Feasible Misunderstanding*. New York: Free Press, 1969.

Murphy, Mark C., ed. *Alasdair MacIntyre*. Cambridge, UK: Cambridge University Press, 2003.

Needleman, Jacob. *The American Soul: Rediscovering the Wisdom of the Founders*. New York: Putnam, 2003.

Niebuhr, Reinhold. *Moral Man and Immoral Society*. Louisville, KY: John Knox Press, 2002.

Niebuhr, Reinhold. *The Legacy of Reinhold Niebuhr*. Edited by Nathan A. Scott. Chicago: University of Chicago Press, 1975.

Niebuhr, Reinhold. *The Essential Reinhold Niebuhr: Selected Essays and Addresses*. Edited by Robert McAfee Brown. New Haven, CT: Yale University Press, 1986.

Nivola, Peitro, and David W. Brady, eds. *Red and Blue Nation?: Characteristics and Causes of America's Polarized Politics*. Washington, DC: Brookings Institution, 2006.

Oakeshott, Michael. *On Human Conduct*. Cambridge: Oxford University Press, 1991.

Oakeshott, Michael. *Rationalism in Politics and Other Essays*. Indianapolis: Liberty Fund, 1991.

Olson, Walter. *The Excuse Factory: How Employment Law Is Paralyzing the American Workplace*. New York: Free Press, 1997.

Olson, Walter. *The Rule of Lawyers*. New York: St. Martin's Press, 2003.

O'Neill, Onora. *A Question of Trust: The BBC Reith Lectures 2002*. Cambridge: Cambridge University Press, 2002.

Osborne, David, and Gaebler, Ted. *Reinventing Government*. New York: Basic Books, 1992.

Paine, Thomas. *Selections*. New York: Hill and Wang, 1961.

Parenti, Michael. *Power and the Powerless*. New York: St. Martin's Press, 1978.

Pestritto, Ronald J., Ed. *Woodrow Wilson: The Essential Political Writings*. Lanham, MD: Lexington Books, 2005.

Peters, Charles. *How Washington Really Works*. New York: Basic Books, 1993.

Peters, Charles, and John Rothchild, eds. *Inside the System*. New York: Praeger, 1975.

Peterson, Peter G. *Running on Empty*. New York: Farrar, Straus and Giroux, 2004.

Polanyi, Michael. *Personal Knowledge: Towards a Post-Critical Philosophy*. Chicago: University of Chicago Press, 1958.

Posner, Richard A. *Overcoming Law*. Cambridge, MA: Harvard University Press, 1995.

Posner, Richard A. *How Judges Think*. Cambridge, MA: Harvard University Press, 2008.

Posner, Richard A., and William M. Landes. *The Economic Structure of Tort Law*. Cambridge, MA: Harvard University Press, 1987.

Postman, Neil. *Technopoly: The Surrender of Culture to Technology*. New York: Vintage, 1993.

Pressman, Jeffrey L., and Aaron Wildavsky. *Implementation: How Great Expectations in Washington Are Dashed in Oakland.* Berkeley: University of California Press, 1984.

Putnam, Robert. *Bowling Alone: America's Declining Social Capital.* New York: Simon & Schuster, 1995.

Putnam, Robert. *Making Democracy Work: Civic Traditions in Modern Italy.* Princeton, NJ: Princeton University Press, 1993.

Putnam, Robert, and Lewis M. Feldstein. *Better Together: Restoring the American Community.* New York: Simon & Schuster, 2003.

Rauch, Jonathan. *Government's End: Why Washington Stopped Working.* New York: Public Affairs, 1999.

Ravitch, Diane. *The Language Police: How Pressure Groups Restrict What Students Learn.* New York: Knopf, 2003.

Ravitch, Diane, and Joseph P. Viteritti. *New Schools for a New Century.* New Haven, CT: Yale University Press, 1997.

Rawls, John. *A Theory of Justice.* Oxford: Oxford University Press, 1999.

Raz, Joseph. *Ethics in the Public Domain: Essays in the Morality of Law and Politics.* Oxford: Clarendon Press, 1995.

Raz, Joseph. *Practical Reason and Norms.* London: Oxford, 1999.

Reisman, William Michael. *Folded Lies: Bribery Crusades and Reforms.* New York: Free Press, 1979.

Rose, Mike. *The Mind at Work: Valuing the Intelligence of the American Worker.* New York: Viking, 2004.

Ross, John F. *The Polar Bear Strategy: Reflections on Risk in Modern Life.* New York: Perseus Books, 1997.

Sandel, Michael, ed. *Liberalism and Its Critics.* New York: New York University Press, 1984.

Sandler, Ross, and David Schoenbrod. *Democracy By Decree: What Happens When Courts Run Government.* New Haven, CT: Yale University Press, 2003.

Schroeder, D. A., ed. *Social Dilemmas.* New York: Praeger, 1995.

Schlesinger, Arthur M., Jr. *The Disuniting of America: Reflections on a Multicultural Society.* New York: W. W. Norton, 1998.

Schlesinger, Arthur M., Jr. *A Life in the 20th Century: Innocent Beginnings, 1917–1950.* Boston: Houghton Mifflin, 2000.

Schuck, Peter H. *Diversity in America: Keeping Government at a Safe Distance.* Cambridge, MA: Belknap, 2006.

Schuck, Peter H., and James Q. Wilson. *Understanding America: The Anatomy of an Exceptional Nation.* New York: Public Affairs, 2008.

Schwartz, Barry. *The Paradox of Choice: Why More Is Less.* New York: HarperCollins, 2005.

Shon, Donald A. *The Reflective Practitioner: How Professionals Think in Action.* New York: Basic Books, 1983.

Shorter, Edward. *Bedside Manners: The Troubled History of Doctors and Patients.* New York: Simon & Schuster, 1985.

Simon, Herbert A. *Reason in Human Affairs*. Palo Alto: Stanford University Press, 1983.

Skiba, Russel, Cecil R. Reynolds, Sandra Graham, Peter Sheras, Jane Close Conoley, and Enedina Garcia-Vazquez. "Are Zero Tolerance Policies Effective in the Schools? An Evidentiary Review and Recommendations." A Report by the American Psychological Association Zero Tolerance Task Force, August 9, 2006.

Skocpol, Theda. *The Missing Middle. New York: The Century Foundation*, 2000.

Smiles, Samuel. *Self Help: With Illustrations of Conduct and Perseverance*. New York: Cosimo Classics, 2005.

Spalding, Matthew, and Patrick Garrity. *A Sacred Union of Citizens: George Washington's Farewell Address and the American Character*. Lanham, MD: Rowman and Littlefield, 1996.

Sternberg, Robert J., George B. Forsythe, Jennifer Hedlund, and Joseph A. Horvath. *Practical Intelligence in Everyday Life*. Cambridge: Cambridge University Press, 2000.

Sternberg, Robert, ed. *Why Smart People Can Be So Stupid*. New Haven, CT: Yale University Press, 2002.

Stillman, Richard J. *Public Administration: Concepts and Cases*. Boston: Houghton Mifflin, 1992.

Sunstein, Cass R. *After the Rights Revolution: Reconceiving the Regulatory State*. Cambridge, MA: Harvard University Press, 1990.

Sunstein, Cass R. *Legal Reasoning and Political Conflict*. New York: Oxford University Press, 1996.

Sunstein, Cass R. *Risk and Reason: Safety, Law, and the Environment*. Cambridge: Cambridge University Press, 2002.

Tainter, Joseph A. *The Collapse of Complex Societies*. Cambridge: Cambridge University Press, 1988.

Taylor, Frederick Winslow. *The Principles of Scientific Management*. New York: W. W. Norton, 1967.

Taylor, Stuart, and KC Johnson. *Until Proven Innocent: Political Correctness and the Shameful Injustices of the Duke Lacrosse Rape Case*. New York: Thomas Dunne Books, 2007.

Terkel, Studs. *My American Century*. New York: New Press, 1997.

Thompson, Dennis. *Restoring Responsibility: Ethics in Government, Business and Healthcare*. Cambridge, UK: Cambridge University Press, 2005.

Trow, George W. S. *Within the Context of No Context*. Boston: Atlantic Monthly Press, 1980.

Turner, Frederick Jackson. *The Frontier in American History*. New York: Henry Holt, 1920.

Useem, Michael. *The Leadership Moment: Nine True Stories of Triumph and Disaster and Their Lessons for Us All*. New York: Random House, 1998.

Van Riper, Paul P. *History of the United States Civil Service*. Westport, CT: Greenwood Press, 1958.

Von Mises, Ludwig. *Bureaucracy*. Grove City, PA: Libertarian Press, 1996.

Vonnegut, Kurt. "Harrison Bergeron," in *Welcome to the Monkey House*. New York: Dial, 1998.

Warren, Mark, ed. *Democracy and Trust*. Cambridge, UK: Cambridge University Press, 1999.

Washington, George. *The Quotable George Washington*. Edited by Stephen E. Lucas. Lanham, MD: Rowman and Littlefield, 1999.

Washington, George. *Writings*. New York: Library of America, 1997.

Weber, Max. *Economy and Society*. Edited by Guenther Roth and Claus Wittich. Berkeley: University of California Press, 1978.

White, Leonard Dupee. *The Federalists: A Study in Administrative History*. New York: Macmillan, 1948.

Whitehead, Alfred North. *An Introduction to Mathematics*. New York: Henry Holt, 1911.

Wildavsky, Aaron. *Searching for Safety*. London: Transaction Books, 1988.

Wills, Gary. *Certain Trumpets: The Nature of Leadership*. New York: Simon & Schuster, 1994.

Wills, Garry. *A Necessary Evil: A History of American Distrust of Government*. New York: Simon & Schuster, 1999.

Wilson, James Q. *Moral Judgment: Does the Abuse Excuse Threaten Our Legal System?* New York: Basic Books, 1997.

Wilson, James Q., and George Kelling. "Broken Windows," *Atlantic Monthly*, March 1982.

Wolfe, Alan. *Return to Greatness: How America Lost Its Sense of Purpose and What It Needs to Do to Recover It*. Princeton, NJ: Princeton University Press, 2005.

Wolfe, Alan. *One Nation, After All*. New York: Viking, 1998.

Wright, Robert. *The Moral Animal: Why We Are the Way We Are; The New Science of Evolutionary Psychology*. New York: Vintage, 1994.

Zakaria, Fareed. The Future of Freedom: *Illiberal Democracy at Home and Abroad*. New York: W. W. Norton, 2003.

Zeigler, Harmon. *The Political Life of Teachers*. Upper Saddle River, NJ: Prentice-Hall, 1967.

ACKNOWLEDGMENTS

I rely unreasonably on friends, family, and colleagues as a sounding board for ideas and for sources. Henry Reath and Tony Kiser were always available to offer encouragement and judgment. Henry Miller at Goodman Media was a trusted adviser and astute reader.

Professor Richard Arum introduced me to the importance of school culture. E. Donald Elliott, lawyer and scholar, was an indispensable resource on the workings of Washington. Bob Litan at the Kauffman Foundation is authoritative, and always available to steer me in the right direction. Dr. Troyen Brennan was a source for issues related to health care; Michelle Mello and David Studdert at The Harvard School of Public Health were rigorous partners in developing ideas for health care justice. Jonathan Rauch at Brookings was generous with his time and ideas. Law professors Ed Dauer, Mary Ann Glendon, Bob Kagan, George Priest, and Peter Schuck were helpful as sounding boards. Steen Lassen and Finn Christenson in Denmark, and Claire Fox and Sir Charles MacLean in the UK, provided useful sources and insights on the workings of law and regulation in other countries. Chris Borreca and Janet Horton at Bracewell Giuliani in Houston helped me understand how special ed laws work in practice. Deborah Brown and Rebecca Urbach walked me through the intricacies of law applied to hospitals. Joe Tanner in Georgia and David Maloney in Florida were wise about the workings of state government. Scores of teachers, doctors, judges, public officials, and others consented to lengthy interviews—thank you all.

My colleagues at Common Good leaned over backwards to help me find sources and materials—Paul Barringer, Sara Berg, Janet Corcoran, Vince Evener, Dina Hasiotis, Ali Kliegman, Andy Park, Mark Schultz, and Franklin Stone. So did Common Good's trustees—Kim Fennebresque, Eric Holder, Marc Lipschultz, Michael Shepherd, Scott Smith, and Missie Rennie Taylor. Members of Common Good's advisory board were always available to open doors and put their reputations behind the need for an overhaul of legal structure—Howard Baker, Griffin Bell, Bill Bradley, Bill Brody, Chris DeMuth, Newt Gingrich, Heather Higgins, Harry Kamen, Charlie Kolb, Larry Mone, Dr. Herbert Pardes, Tom Kean, Diane Ravitch, Dr. Jack Rowe, Alan Simpson, Larry Thompson, and Deborah Wadsworth made themselves and their rolodexes available whenever needed. Supporters of Common Good provided more than trust and resources—Julian Robertson and Bill Goodell, and Risa Lavizzo-Mourey, Nancy Barrand, and others at The Robert Wood Johnson Foundation, stand out as entrepreneurs of philanthropy. My friends hold on to their wallets when they see me coming, but they're a soft touch and have made possible the projects described in this book.

My colleagues at Covington & Burling offered their expertise and judgment about the workings of Washington—particularly Rod DeArment and Marty Gold. Covington has an extraordinary history and culture of public service, and I thank all my colleagues for accommodating my passion here.

Research help was indispensable, and five recent Yale graduates formed a kind of tag team to help me find, and check, ideas and sources. Jonas Oransky became a scholar of political philosophy, devoting almost three years to the issues described in this book.

Brad Lipton has unique analytical skills and was insightful as a reader of early drafts. Morgan Babst brought her writer's eye and sharp intelligence to the final year of work. Aryeh Cohen-Wade helped at the end when others were unavailable. Alan Rosinus started it all off in 2003. Other research help was provided by Gina Merrill, who researched the paper for the 2005 Lawsuits and Liberty conference at the National Constitution Center, and by Paul Devlin, who helped with certain historical material.

Simon Head and my daughter Charlotte Howard read early sketches and kicked around ideas. Kent Barwick, Philippa Dunne, Ron Faucheux, Ken Godat, Jonathan Slonim, Simon Brantler, and Nolan Reichl were close readers. Richard Boulware helped me negotiate the shoals of political sensitivity. Richard Nash Gould made sure I was aware of the arguments for political insensitivity. My brothers John Allen and Bobby Howard acted as a clipping service from the South. Bob Dilenschneider, Michael Donovan, Shelley Wanger, Paul Soulellis, Mary Reath, and many others advised on the title.

My agent Andrew Wylie continues to be an indispensable resource, not only placing and promoting the book but also putting his reputation on the line for these ideas. My editor, Starling Lawrence at W. W. Norton, has a gift for spotting holes and weak points, and helped make the final product measurably better. The rest of the team at W. W. Norton has been smart and thankfully unbureaucratic—I particularly thank Louise Brockett, Elizabeth Riley, and Nydia Parries.

Arthur M. Schlesinger, Jr., regularly volunteered ideas and sources for my work, and encouraged me even when he (and I) did not know where it might lead. I miss him.

Finally, my family has been a source of strength and support throughout. My children Olivia, Charlotte, Lily, and Alexander, and son-in-law Ernie Sabine, were an involuntary focus group—I value the judgment of each of them. Alexandra let me be, and shouldered loads that should have been mine. Thank you.

ABOUT THE AUTHOR

Philip K. Howard, a lawyer, is a leading advocate of legal reform. He is the author of *The Death of Common Sense* and founder of Common Good (www.commongood.org). As a civic leader in New York, Howard chaired the committee that installed the "Tribute in Light" memorial to victims at the World Trade Center.